Idea in Brief

Many companies fail to se
opportunities hidden in e
downturns.

To take advantage of opportunities, you first need to do a thorough but rapid assessment of your
own vulnerabilities and then move
decisively to minimize them.

or transformative acquisitions.

---

borrow reduce demand for your products? Will job insecurity and
deflating asset prices make even the creditworthy increasingly
reluctant to take on more debt? Will reduced demand affect your
ability to secure short-term financing, or will weak stock markets
make it difficult to raise equity? Even if you are able to tap the debt
and equity markets, will higher borrowing costs and return requirements raise your cost of capital?

Quantify the impact on your business
Run simulations for each of these scenarios that generate financial
outcomes on the basis of major variables, including sales volume,
prices, and variable costs. Be sure to confront head on what you see
as the worst case. For example, what effect would a 20% decline in
sales volume and a 5% decline in prices have on your overall financial
performance? You may be surprised to find out that, even in the case
of a still-healthy company with operating margins (before interest
and taxes) of around 10%, such a decline in volume and prices could
turn current profits into huge losses and send cash flow deep into
the red. Conduct a similar analysis for each business unit.

Next, quantify how your balance sheet might be affected under
the different scenarios. For example, what will the impact be of
asset price deflation? To what extent might lower cash flows and the
higher cost of capital affect goodwill and require write-offs on past
acquisitions? Will falling commodity prices cushion some of the det-
rimental effects?

Idea in Practice

Before trying to capitalize on the opportunities presented by a recession, you must assess and minimize your firm's vulnerabilities. The authors suggest setting up a recession checklist.

Financial Fundamentals

Liquidity is the key to surviving and thriving in tough times, when both cash to meet current obligations and capital for investing in the future are scarce. So you need to . . .

Monitor and maximize your cash position

- Calculate expected cash inflows and outflows
- Produce a rolling weekly or monthly cash report
- Centralize or pool cash across units

Tightly manage customer credit

- Segment customers based on their credit risk
- Offer financing only to credit-worthy or strategic customers
- Assess trade-offs between credit risks and marginal sales

Aggressively manage working capital

- Reduce inventories by monitoring production and sourcing
- Reduce receivables by actively managing customer credit

Optimize your financial structure

- Reduce debt and other liabilities
- Secure access to lines of credit
- Secure access to equity capital by tapping nonmarket sources such as sovereign wealth funds

Share Price

A strong market valuation relative to rivals is important in raising capital and acting on acquisition opportunities. So you need to . . .

- Inform investors and analysts of your recession preparedness
- Consider opting for dividend payments rather than share buybacks

Assess rivals' vulnerabilities

Of course, none of this process should be carried out in a vacuum. Your industry and the locations of your operations around the world will help determine how your business will be affected. It's critical to understand your own strengths and weaknesses relative to those of your competitors. They will have different cost structures,

HBR'S 10 MUST READS

EXPANDED EDITION

On
Managing in
a Downturn

HBR's 10 Must Reads series is the definitive collection of ideas and best practices for aspiring and experienced leaders alike. These books offer essential reading selected from the pages of *Harvard Business Review* on topics critical to the success of every manager.

Titles include:

HBR'S 10 MUST READS

EXPANDED EDITION

On Managing in a Downturn

HARVARD BUSINESS REVIEW PRESS

Boston, Massachusetts

Copyright 2020 Harvard Business School Publishing Corporation

All rights reserved
Printed in the United States of America
10 9 8 7 6 5 4 3 2 1

No part of this publication may be reproduced, stored in or introduced into a retrieval system, or transmitted, in any form, or by any means (electronic, mechanical, photocopying, recording, or otherwise), without the prior permission of the publisher. Requests for permission should be directed to permissions@harvardbusiness.org, or mailed to Permissions, Harvard Business School Publishing, 60 Harvard Way, Boston, Massachusetts 02163.

The web addresses referenced in this book were live and correct at the time of the book's publication but may be subject to change.

Cataloging-in-Publication data is forthcoming.

The paper used in this publication meets the requirements of the American National Standard for Permanence of Paper for Publications and Documents in Libraries and Archives Z39.48-1992.

ISBN: 978-1-64782-065-7
eISBN: 978-1-64782-066-4

Contents

**HBR'S
10
MUST
READS**

On
**Managing in
a Downturn**

EXPANDED
EDITION

Seize Advantage in a Downturn

by David Rhodes and Daniel Stelter

INACTION IS THE RISKIEST RESPONSE to the uncertainties of an economic crisis. But rash or scattershot action can be nearly as damaging. Rising anxiety (how much worse are things likely to get? how long is this going to last?) and the growing pressure to do *something* often produces a variety of uncoordinated moves that target the wrong problem or overshoot the right one. A disorganized response can also generate a sense of panic in an organization. And that will distract people from seeing something crucially important: the hidden but significant opportunities nestled among the bad economic news.

We offer here a rapid but measured approach—simultaneously defensive and offensive—to tackling the challenges posed by a downturn. Many companies are already engaged in some kind of exercise like this. Certainly every organization with an institutional pulse has held discussions focusing on what it should do about the current economic crisis. We hope this article will help you move from what may have been ad hoc conversations and initiatives to a carefully thought-out plan.

The merits of a comprehensive and aggressive approach are borne out in research by the Boston Consulting Group, which indicates that companies whose early responses to a downturn are tentative (for example, modest belt-tightening) typically overreact later on (say, cutting costs more than they ultimately need to). This results in an expensive recovery for the company when the economy rebounds.

1

Our approach has two main objectives, from which a series of action items devolves. First, stabilize your business, protecting it from downside risk and ensuring that it has the liquidity necessary to weather the crisis. Then, and only then, can you identify ways to capitalize on the downturn in the longer term, partly by exploiting the mistakes of less savvy rivals.

For some companies, the outcome of this process will be a program of immediate actions that represent a turbocharged version of business as usual. For others, it will be a painful realization that nothing short of an urgent corporate turnaround will suffice.

What Is Your Exposure?

The first step for a company to take in a challenging economic environment—especially one that could significantly worsen—is to assess in a systematic manner its own vulnerabilities, at the company level and by business unit.

Consider several scenarios

As an economic crisis evolves, sketch out at least three scenarios— a modest downturn, a more severe recession, and a full-blown depression, as defined by both duration and severity. Consider which scenario is most likely to unfold in your industry and your business, based on available data and analysis. There was evidence from the beginning, for example, that the current global downturn truly stands apart. Early on, banking losses had outstripped those of recent financial disasters, including the United States savings and loan crisis (1986-1995), the Japanese banking crisis (1990-1999), and the Asian financial crisis (1998-1999). Furthermore, as the economy first began to stall, the underlying problem of consumer and corporate indebtedness—in the United States, it totaled about 380% of GDP, nearly two and a half times the level at the beginning of the Great Depression—pointed to a prolonged period of economic pain.

Next, determine the ways in which each of the scenarios might affect your business. How would consumers' limited capacity to

Current Business

Loosely run operations, sluggish unit sales, and an overextended enterprise leave you vulnerable to economic shocks. So you need to . . .

Reduce costs and increase efficiency

- Root out long-standing activities that add little business value

- Revive earlier efficiency initiatives too controversial to fully implement in better times

- Consolidate or centralize key functions

- Analyze current suppliers and procurement practices

- Reexamine the economics of offshoring

Aggressively manage the top line

- Revitalize customer retention initiatives

- Realign sales force utilization and incentives to generate additional short-term revenue

- Reallocate marketing spending toward immediate revenue generation

- Consider more-generous financial terms for customers in return for higher prices

Rethink your product mix and pricing strategies

- Offer lower-price versions of existing products

- Identify products for which customers are still willing to pay full price

- Consider creative strategies such as results-based or subscription pricing

- Unbundle services and adopt à la carte pricing

Rein in planned investments and sell assets

- Establish stringent capital allocation guidelines

- Shed unproductive assets that were difficult to dispose of in good times

- Divest noncore businesses

financial positions, sourcing strategies, product mixes, customer focuses, and so on. To emerge from the downturn in a lead position, you must calibrate the actions you plan to take in light of the actions that your competitors will most likely take. For example, assess potential acquisitions with a focus on vulnerable customer groups of weaker competitors.

This assessment of different scenarios and their effects on your company and its rivals, while just a first step, will help you identify particular areas where you're vulnerable and where action is most immediately needed. This analysis will also help you to communicate to the entire organization the justification and the motivation for actions you'll need to take in response to the crisis.

How Can You Reduce Your Exposure?

Once you understand how your business could be affected, you need to figure out the best way to survive and maximize your company's performance during the downturn. This requires achieving several broad objectives.

Protect the financial fundamentals

The aim here is to ensure that your company has adequate cash flow and access to capital. Not only does a lack of liquidity create immediate problems but it also is critically important to your ability to make smart investments in the future of the business.

Consequently, you need to *monitor and maximize your cash position*, by using a disciplined cash management system, by reducing or postponing spending, and by focusing on cash inflow. Produce a rolling report on your cash position (either weekly or monthly, depending on the volatility of your business) that details expected near-term payments and receipts. Also estimate how your cash position is likely to evolve in the midterm, calculating expected cash inflows and outflows. You may need to establish a centralized cash management system that provides companywide data and enables pooling of cash across business units.

How much spending you postpone depends on your assumptions about the severity of the downturn and to what degree such spending is discretionary. But you'll want to be just as aggressive in looking for ways to improve cash flow—if you were facing a worst-case-scenario liquidity crisis, for example, just how much cash would you be able to raise during the next quarter?

One way to improve cash flow is to more aggressively *manage customer credit risk*. Trade credit—financing your customers' purchases by letting them pay over time—should be reduced where possible. Given the economic environment, buyers will seek credit more frequently and your risk will increase. You'll need to segment your customers by assigning them each a credit rating. Avoid granting trade credit to higher-risk customers or to those whose business is less strategically important to you. Also, assess the trade-off between credit risks and the revenue potential of a marginal sale. This will require cooperation between people in sales and customer finance, as well as a review of those employees' incentives to make sure they're aligned with revised strategic goals for the downturn.

Another way to free up cash is to look for opportunities to *reduce working capital*. A surprisingly large number of companies are unaware of the benefits of aggressively managing their working capital—the difference between a company's current assets and liabilities—and thus make little effort to even monitor it. As a rule of thumb, most manufacturing companies can free up cash equivalent to approximately 10% of sales by optimizing their working capital. This involves reducing current assets, such as inventories (through more careful management of both production and sourcing processes) and receivables (through, in part, the active management of trade credit).

As you scrutinize your customers' debt profiles, you should review your own as well, in order to *optimize your financial structure and financing options*. The heyday of leverage, with constant pressure from the market to operate with relatively low levels of equity, is clearly over for now. You should be looking for ways to strengthen your balance sheet, reducing debt and other liabilities, such as operating leases or pension obligations, with the dual aim of reducing your financial risk and enhancing your risk profile in the eyes of investors.

Be sure, as well, to secure financing—for example, draw on lines of credit as soon as possible to provide liquidity for day-to-day operations, holding onto any excess cash to avoid refinancing problems in the future. Meeting such needs may require some creativity in a tight credit market. For example, some companies, in renewing revolving credit facilities with banks, have agreed to forgo fixed interest rates on the funds they draw down under the facility. Instead, borrowers have agreed to link the rate to the trading price of their so-called credit default swaps. These financial instruments, which represent a form of insurance against a borrower defaulting, reflect the market's perception of a company's creditworthiness. By agreeing to initially high and variable interest rates for a line of credit, borrowing companies can secure access to funds at a time when skittish banks are reluctant to lend. To secure equity capital, companies need to look beyond the market to sources such as sovereign wealth funds, private equity firms, or cash-rich investors.

Protect the existing business

After ensuring that the company is on a firm financial footing, turn to protecting the viability of the business. You must be prepared to act quickly and decisively to improve core operations.

Begin with aggressive moves to *reduce costs and increase efficiency*. Although cost-cutting is the first thing most companies think about, their actions are often tentative and conservative. You need to work rapidly to implement measures, using the turbulent economic environment to catalyze action that is long overdue—or to revive earlier initiatives that proved too controversial to fully implement in good times. Keep in mind, though, that while speed is important so is a well-reasoned plan: You don't want to make cuts that in the long term will hurt more than they help by, for example, putting important future business opportunities at risk.

Some means of streamlining the organization and lowering break-even points are obvious: stripping out layers of the organizational hierarchy to reduce head count, consolidating or centralizing key functions, discontinuing long-standing but low-value-added activities. SG&A expenses—selling, general, and administrative costs, such as marketing—are also prime targets for cost-cutting. As such, they can highlight the risks of purely reactive action: Companies that injudiciously slash marketing spending often find that they later must spend far more than they saved in order to recover from their prolonged absence from the media landscape.

Opportunities to reduce materials and supply chain costs also arise in a downturn. Now is the time to pursue a comprehensive review of your current suppliers and procurement practices, which undoubtedly will prompt new initiatives—the adoption of a demand management system, say, or the standardization of components. In particular, consider how the downturn affects the economic equation of offshore manufacturing. Falling shipping costs could make offshoring more attractive, even for low-cost items; at the same time, a weakening domestic currency, trade barriers, and especially the cash tied up in the additional working capital required to source a product far from its market may offset any savings.

While looking for opportunities to reduce spending, you'll also want to *aggressively manage the top line,* cash being crucially important in a recession. Actively work both to protect existing revenue and identify ways to generate additional revenue from your current business. Customer retention initiatives become more valuable than ever. Consider tactical changes in sales force utilization and incentives. Reallocate marketing spending to bolster immediate revenue generation rather than longer-term brand building. While granting trade credit sparingly, also consider the possible benefits of offering customers more-generous financial terms while charging them higher prices—provided you've done your homework on your own financial structure.

As these initiatives suggest, you'll want to *rethink your product mix and pricing strategies* in response to shifting customer needs. Purchasing behavior changes dramatically in a recession. Consumers increasingly opt for lower-priced alternatives to their usual purchases, trading down to buy private label products or to shop at discount retailers. Although some consumers will continue to trade up, they'll do so in smaller numbers and in fewer categories. Consumer products companies should consider offering low-priced versions of popular products—think of the McDonald's Dollar Menu in the United States or Danone's Eco-Pack yogurt in France. Whatever your business, determine how the needs, preferences, and spending patterns of your customers, whether consumer or corporate, are affected by the economic climate. For example, careful segmentation may reveal products primarily purchased by people still willing to pay full price. Use that intelligence to inform product portfolio and investment choices.

Innovative pricing strategies may also alleviate downward pressure on revenue. These include: results-based pricing, a concept pioneered by consulting firms that links payment to measurable customer benefits resulting from use of a product or service; changes in the pricing basis that would allow a customer to, for example, rent equipment by the hour rather than by the day; subscription pricing, by which a customer purchases use of a product—say, a machine tool—rather than the product itself; and the unbundling of a service so that customers pay separately for different elements of what was previously an all-in-one package, as airlines have done with checked baggage and in-flight meals and entertainment. Offering consumers new and creative customer financing packages could tip the balance in favor of a sale. It was during the Great Depression, after all, that GE developed its innovative strategy of financing customers' refrigerator purchases.

You should definitely *rein in your investment program*. Most developed economies had excess capacity even before the downturn: Capacity utilization in the United States, for example, fell below 80% of potential output beginning in April 2008. In the current economy, there is even less need, in most industries, to invest in further capacity. You need to establish stringent capital allocation guidelines aligned with the current economic climate, if you haven't already. This may also be the time to shed unproductive assets, including manufacturing plants that have previously been difficult to shut down, selling them where possible to generate cash for the business.

Finally, take this opportunity to *divest noncore businesses*, selling off peripheral or poorly performing operations. Don't wait for better times, in the hope of getting a price that matches those of recent years, when the economy was buoyant and credit was plentiful. Those conditions aren't likely to return anytime soon, and if the

Avoiding the Snags of Implementation

ONE KEY TO THE SUCCESS of downturn-related initiatives is rapid implementation. A formal crisis management team to oversee your company's response to the recession can help the organization avoid these typical sources of failure.

Insufficient understanding and appreciation of the evolving crisis

The crisis management team can help create and maintain a sense of urgency within the organization, in part by creating a transparent, consistent, and fact-based process for carrying out the necessary initiatives. The team should also continually monitor the economic situation and, if needed, move from, say, a modest downturn scenario to a worst-case action plan.

Senior leaders' lack of preparation and commitment

By promoting a close working relationship with the sponsor of the company's recession response (often the CEO), the team can keep the company's senior executives informed of progress and direct them to where their participation is needed.

Failure to see how individual initiatives are part of a comprehensive plan

By establishing the priority and timing of initiatives, the team can help ensure that the individual measures reinforce one another. The team should continually evaluate initiatives both individually and collectively, with the aim of suspending, accelerating, or combining existing efforts—or initiating new ones.

Lack of attention to the human element

To earn employees' commitment to the initiatives, the team must articulate the threats facing the organization, explain why change is needed and what it will entail, and clearly communicate to individuals how they will be affected.

business isn't critical to your activities and increases your vulnerability to the downturn, divest it now.

Research by our firm shows a strongly positive market reaction to the right divestitures in recessionary times. And shedding non-core operations ideally will end up energizing your core business. In 2003, in the middle of a particularly acute economic downturn in Germany, MG Technologies, a €6.4 billion engineering and chemicals company, decided to focus on its specialty mechanical engineering business. It sold its noncore chemical and plant engineering businesses and emerged as the renamed GEA Group, a slimmed down but successful specialty process engineering and equipment company, better positioned to pursue growth opportunities in its core areas.

Maximize your valuation relative to rivals

Your company's share price, like that of most firms, will take a beating during a downturn. While you may not be able to prevent it from dropping in absolute terms, you want it to remain strong compared with others in your industry. Much of what you've done to protect the financial fundamentals of your business will serve you well. In a downturn, our data shows that markets typically reward a strong balance sheet with low debt levels and secured access to capital. Instead of being punished by activist investors and becoming a takeover target for hedge funds, a company sitting on a pile of cash is viewed positively by investors as a stable investment with lower perceived risk. For that to happen, you need to *create a compelling investor communications strategy* that highlights such drivers of relative valuation. This will also be important as you try to capitalize on the competitive opportunities that a recession offers, such as seeking attractive mergers and acquisitions.

You can further enhance your relative value if you *reassess your dividend policy and share buyback plans*. A Boston Consulting Group study of U.S. public companies found that, on average, investors favor dividends because they represent a much stronger financial commitment to investors than buybacks, which can be stopped at any time without serious consequences. On average, sustained dividend increases of 25% or more overwhelmingly resulted in higher relative valuation multiples in the two quarters following their announcement. By contrast, buybacks had almost no impact on the relative valuation multiple in the two quarters following the transaction. For example, TJX Companies, a U.S. discount retailer, announced a dividend increase of 33% in June 2002, when the country was in a recession—and then enjoyed a price-to-earnings multiple 42% higher than the average of S&P 500 companies over the two quarters following the announcement. These are exceptional times, though, and we recommend that companies analyze their particular situation as well as investor preferences before taking a specific measure.

How Can You Gain Long-Term Advantage?

The best companies do more than survive a downturn. They position themselves to thrive during the subsequent upturn, guided again by a number of broad objectives.

Invest for the future

Investments made today in areas such as product development and information or production technology will, in many cases, bear fruit only after the recession is past. Waiting to move forward with such investments may compromise your ability to capitalize on opportunities when the economy rebounds. And the cost of these investments will be lower now, as competition for resources slackens.

Given current financial constraints, you won't be able to do everything, of course, or even most things. But that shouldn't keep you from making some big bets. Prioritize the different options, protecting investments likely to have a major impact on the long-term health of the company, delaying ones with less-certain positive outcomes, and ditching those projects that would be nice to have but aren't crucial to future success.

Sanofi-Synthélabo, the French pharmaceutical company, entered the economic recession that began in 2001 with a solid product portfolio. Throughout the downturn, the company maintained, and in some cases increased, its R&D spending in order to keep its product pipeline robust. Sanofi increased its absolute R&D expenditure from €950 million in 2000 to €1.3 billion in 2003. Because of its strong business and financial performance, the company gained market share and outperformed peers in the stock market. The company was thus well positioned to acquire Aventis, a much larger Franco-German pharmaceutical company, after a takeover battle, in the economic upswing of 2004.

Or look at Apple Computer. The company wasn't in particularly good shape as it headed into the 2001–2003 recession. For one thing, revenue fell 33% in 2001 over the previous year. Nonetheless, Apple increased its R&D expenditures by 13% in 2001—to roughly 8% of sales from less than 5% in 2000—and maintained that level in the following two years. The result: Apple introduced the iTunes music store and software in 2003 and the iPod Mini and the iPod Photo in 2004, setting off a period of rapid growth for the company.

A downturn is also a good time to invest in people—for example, to upgrade the quality of your management teams. Competition for top people will be less fierce, availability higher, and the cost correspondingly lower.

Pursue opportunistic and transformative M&A

The recession will change several of the long-standing rules of the game in many industries. Exploit your competitors' vulnerabilities to redefine your industry through consolidation. History shows that the best deals are made in downturns. According to research by our firm, downturn mergers generate about 15% more value, as measured by total shareholder return, than boom-time mergers, which on average exhibit negative TSR.

To capitalize on opportunities, closely monitor the financial and operational health of your competitors. Companies lacking the financial cushion to benefit from the recession—or even to stay afloat—may even welcome your advances.

In late 2001, only weeks after the 9/11 terrorist attacks had brought vacation travel to a near standstill, Carnival, the world's largest cruise ship operator, interceded in the planned friendly merger of Royal Caribbean and P&O Princess Cruises, then the second and third largest cruise operations respectively. Its own bid to acquire P&O Princess required persistence—it was 15 months before P&O Princess shareholders finally accepted Carnival's offer—but the deal turned out to be a smart strategic move for the company, whose total shareholder returns far surpassed those of the S&P 500 in the years following the announcement and then the completion of the acquisition.

Of course, you'll have to ride out the recession carrying the baggage of any company you acquire, so due diligence—particularly concerning a potential target's current and future cash positions—takes on even more importance during a downturn. This knowledge will help you to limit the particular risks arising from an acquisition made during a recession, as well as to convince your management teams and supervisory boards that a bold move during a period of caution makes sense.

Rethink your business models

Downturns can be a time of wrenching transformation for companies and industries. The economics of the business may change because of increased competition, changing input costs, government intervention, or new trade policies. New competitors and business models may emerge as companies seek to increase revenue through expansion into adjacent product categories or horizontal integration. Successful companies will anticipate these changes to the industry landscape and adapt their business models ahead of the competition to protect the existing business and to gain advantage.

Consider IBM. During the U.S. recession of the early 1990s, the company under Lou Gerstner faced its first decline in revenue since 1940 and endured successive years of record losses. In this context, it began to rethink its business model. Struggling with sluggish economic growth, particularly in Europe and Japan, as well as increased price competition, IBM was forced to confront head on the inevitable decline of its traditional business, mainframe computers. Realizing that the company's markets were shifting, Gerstner redefined the company's business model, transforming IBM from a hardware producer into a computer services and solutions provider.

Where Do You Take Action?

The process we have laid out should yield a list of promising initiatives—undoubtedly more of them than you'll have the capacity to launch and manage all at once. So you'll need to prioritize, carefully assessing each initiative based on several criteria—most notably, urgency, overall financial impact, barriers to implementation, and risks that the initiative might pose for the business. The result will be a portfolio of actions with the right blend of short-term and long-term focus.

Who is going to carry out the recession plan? We recommend that you form a dedicated crisis management team to manage your organization's response to the recession. The team will develop different economic scenarios and determine how they might affect the business; identify recession-related risks and opportunities; and prioritize initiatives designed to mitigate the risks and capitalize on the opportunities. It will then oversee implementation of the initiatives, monitoring their progress and continually reevaluating them in the light of changes in the economic landscape. (For a summary of how the crisis management team can help ensure a recession plan's success, see the sidebar "Avoiding the Snags of Implementation.")

Companies adopting the comprehensive approach we have laid out will be not only better placed to weather the current storm but also primed to seize the opportunities emerging from the turbulence and to get a head start on the competition as the dark clouds begin to disperse.

Originally published in February 2009. Reprint R0902C

How to Survive a Recession and Thrive Afterward

A Research Roundup. *by Walter Frick*

IN EARLY 2000, A FIVE-YEAR-OLD online bookseller called Amazon
.com sold $672 million in convertible bonds to shore up its finan-
cial position. One month later, the dot-com bubble burst. More than
half of all digital startups went out of business over the next few
years—including lots of Amazon's then-rivals in e-commerce. Had
the bubble burst just a few weeks earlier, one of the most successful
companies ever might have fallen victim to that recession.

Recessions—defined as two consecutive quarters of negative
economic growth—can be caused by economic shocks (such as a
spike in oil prices), financial panics (like the one that preceded the
Great Recession), rapid changes in economic expectations (the so-
called "animal spirits" described by John Maynard Keynes; this is
what caused the dot-com bubble to burst), or some combination of
the three. Most firms suffer during a recession, primarily because
demand (and revenue) falls and uncertainty about the future
increases. But research shows that there are ways to mitigate the
damage.

In their 2010 HBR article "Roaring Out of Recession," Ranjay
Gulati, Nitin Nohria, and Franz Wohlgezogen found that during the
recessions of 1980, 1990, and 2000, 17% of the 4,700 public companies they studied fared particularly badly: They went bankrupt,

went private, or were acquired. But just as striking, 9% of the companies didn't simply recover in the three years after a recession—they flourished, outperforming competitors by at least 10% in sales and profits growth. A more recent analysis by Bain using data from the Great Recession reinforced that finding. The top 10% of companies in Bain's analysis saw their earnings climb steadily throughout the period and continue to rise afterward. A third study, by McKinsey, found similar results.

The difference maker was preparation. Among the companies that stagnated in the aftermath of the Great Recession, "few made contingency plans or thought through alternative scenarios," according to the Bain report. "When the downturn hit, they switched to survival mode, making deep cuts and reacting defensively." Many of the companies that merely limp through a recession are slower to recover and never really catch up.

How should a company prepare in advance of a recession and what moves should it make when one hits? Research and case studies examining the Great Recession shed light on those questions. In some cases, they cement conventional wisdom; in others, they challenge it. Some of the most interesting findings deal with four areas: debt, decision making, workforce management, and digital transformation. The underlying message across all areas is that recessions are a high-pressure exercise in change management, and to navigate one successfully, a company needs to be flexible and ready to adjust.

Deleverage Before a Downturn

Rebecca Henderson (of Harvard Business School) likes to remind her students, "Rule one is: Don't crash the company." That means, first and foremost, don't run out of money. Because a recession usually brings lower sales and therefore less cash to fund operations, surviving a downturn requires deft financial management. If Amazon hadn't raised all that money prior to the dot-com bust, its options would have been much more limited. Instead, it was able to absorb losses in its investments in other startups and also launch Amazon Marketplace, its platform for third-party sellers, later that year. It further expanded during and after the recession into new segments (kitchens, travel, and apparel) and markets (Canada).

Companies with high levels of debt are especially vulnerable during a recession, studies show. In a 2017 study, Xavier Giroud (of MIT's Sloan School of Management) and Holger Mueller (of NYU's Stern School of Business) looked at the relationship between business closures and associated unemployment and falling housing prices in various U.S. counties. Overall, the more housing prices declined, the more consumer demand fell, driving increased business closures and higher unemployment. But the researchers found that this effect was most pronounced among companies with the highest levels of debt. They divided up companies on the basis of whether they became more or less leveraged in the run-up to the recession, as measured by the change in their debt-to-assets ratio. The vast majority of businesses that shuttered because of falling demand were highly leveraged.

"The more debt you have, the more cash you need to make your interest and principal payment," Mueller explains. When a recession hits and less cash is coming in the door, "it puts you at risk of defaulting." To keep up with payments, companies with more debt are forced to cut costs more aggressively, often through layoffs. These deep cuts can impair their productivity and ability to fund new investments. Leverage effectively limits companies' options, forcing their hand and leaving them little room to act opportunistically.

The extent to which high levels of debt pose a risk during a recession depends on various factors. Shai Bernstein (of the Stanford Graduate School of Business), Josh Lerner (of Harvard Business School), and Filippo Mezzanotti (of Northwestern University's Kellogg School of Management) have found that companies owned by private equity firms—which often require the companies they finance to take on debt—fared better during the Great Recession than similarly leveraged non-PE-owned firms. Companies with lots of debt struggle in part because access to capital slows to a trickle during a downturn. PE-backed firms emerged in better shape, the study suggests, because their owners were able to help them raise capital when they needed it. Issuing equity is another way companies

Companies That Prepare for a Recession Pull Ahead During and After It

by Mark Kovac and Jamie Cleghorn

RECESSIONS CATCH MANY COMPANIES by surprise, with predictable results. In the 2001 recession, total sales for the S&P 500 declined by 9% from its prerecession peak to its trough 18 months later—almost a year after

Companies that prepare for a recession pull ahead during and after it

Aggregated average EBIT indexed to 2003

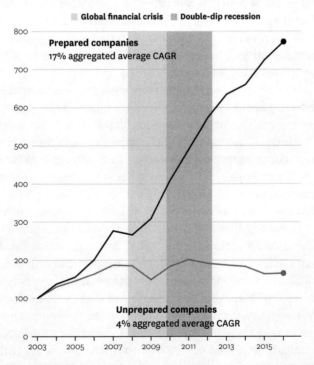

Source: Bain analysis of Capital IQ data. Includes 388 prepared companies and 3,113 unprepared companies worldwide.

Note: A double-dip recession is when GDP becomes negative after at least a quarter of positive growth. EBIT and CAGR are not adjusted for inflation.

the recession officially ended. But these periods also present opportunities for well-prepared companies to take advantage of the turmoil and gain share.

The best time to undertake major changes that will strengthen a company during recession is before it hits. Prior to the past recession, both eventual winners and eventual losers in a group of 3,500 companies worldwide experienced double-digit growth rates. Once the recession struck, however, performance began to diverge sharply—the winners continued to grow while losers stalled out. The performance gap widened during the recovery. What did the winners do that losers didn't? They pursued a variety of tactics *before* the recession that were designed to fortify the firm when the downturn hit.

Mark Kovac is a partner with Bain & Company's Customer Strategy & Marketing practice and leads the firm's B2B Commercial Excellence group. **Jamie Cleghorn** is a partner with Bain & Company's Customer Strategy & Marketing practice.

Adapted from Mark Kovac and Jamie Cleghorn, "What Sales Teams Should Do to Prepare for a Recession," hbr.org, November 23, 2018.

can avoid the burden of debt obligations. "If you issue equity in the run-up to a recession," Mueller says, "the problem of defaulting will be less pronounced."

The reality, of course, is that many companies have some level of debt going into a recession. Mueller's study found that the average debt-to-assets ratio among firms that had increased debt levels in the run-up to the Great Recession was 38.3%. Among the group that had deleveraged, it was 19.5%. Although there's no magic number, modest levels of debt aren't necessarily a problem, research shows. Nonetheless, Mueller suggests that if a company thinks a recession is coming, it should consider deleveraging. McKinsey's recent recession research supports this: Firms that emerged in better shape from the Great Recession had reduced their leverage more dramatically from 2007 to 2011 than had less successful ones.

When it comes to deleveraging, it helps to start early, says McKinsey's Mihir Mysore. That means reducing debt levels before it's clear the economy is in recession. "You need to take a hard look at your portfolio," Mysore advises, because shedding assets can be a way to reduce leverage without necessarily cutting core aspects of operations.

Focus on Decision Making

A company's performance during and after a recession depends not just on the decisions it makes but also on who makes them. In a 2017 study, Raffaella Sadun (of Harvard Business School), Philippe Aghion (of Collège de France), Nicholas Bloom and Brian Lucking (of Stanford), and John Van Reenen (of MIT) examined how organizational structure affects a company's ability to navigate downturns. On the one hand, "the need to make tough decisions may favor centralized firms," the researchers write, because they have a better picture of the organization as a whole and their incentives are typically more closely aligned with company performance. On the other hand, decentralized firms may be better positioned to weather macro shocks "because the value of local information increases."

The researchers relied on data from the World Management Survey of manufacturers, which includes questions on how much autonomy a plant manager has to make investments, introduce new products, make sales and marketing decisions, and hire employees. Companies in which plant managers had little discretion were considered highly centralized; those in which they had a lot of discretion were scored as less so. The researchers also examined results from a similar survey run by the U.S. Census and matched them with company reports of sales, employment levels, profits, and other performance measures. And they gathered data on which industries were hardest hit by the Great Recession. "Decentralization was associated with relatively better performance for firms or establishments facing the toughest environment during the crisis," the researchers report. They also found that the benefits of decentralization faded as economic conditions improved—a sign that delegation has particular value during uncertain times.

Why did decentralization help? "The recession introduced a lot of uncertainty and turbulence," says Sadun. Because decentralized firms delegated decision making further down the hierarchy, they were better able to adapt to changing conditions. For example, they were more aggressive in adjusting their product offerings in response to changes in demand. "One [piece of] advice would be [to] really think carefully about your organizational structure because that's one way you cope with uncertainty," says Sadun.

Of course, organizational structure isn't easy to adjust quickly in preparation for a recession, but that doesn't mean companies can't learn from these findings. "What decentralization does," says Sadun, "is match decisions with expertise." She says companies can fall into the trap of hoarding decision rights during a downturn. But the uncertainty of a recession necessitates experimentation, which requires that decisions be made throughout the organization. Even if companies decide not to decentralize, they can try to do a better job of gathering input from employees at all levels when making key decisions. "Recessions offer opportunities for change," notes Sadun.

Look Beyond Layoffs

Some layoffs are inevitable in a downturn; during the Great Recession, 2.1 million Americans were laid off in 2009 alone. However, the companies that emerged from the crisis in the strongest shape relied less on layoffs to cut costs and leaned more on operational improvements, Ranjay Gulati and his colleagues found in their study of public companies.

That's because layoffs aren't just harmful to workers; they're costly for companies, too. Hiring and training are expensive, so companies prefer not to have to rehire when the economy picks back up, particularly if they think the downturn will be brief. Layoffs can also hurt morale, dampening productivity at a time when companies can ill afford it.

Fortunately, layoffs aren't the only way to cut labor costs. Companies should consider hour reductions, furloughs, and performance pay. After the stock market crash in 2000, Honeywell laid off nearly 20% of its workforce and then struggled to recover in the downturn that followed. So when the Great Recession hit, in 2008, the company took a different approach, as Sandra J. Sucher and Shalene Gupta describe in their 2018 HBR article, "Layoffs That Don't Break Your Company." "Honeywell furloughed employees for one to five weeks, providing unpaid or partially compensated leaves, depending on local labor regulations," Sucher and Gupta wrote. That saved an estimated 20,000 jobs. Honeywell emerged from the Great Recession in better shape than it did from the 2000 recession in terms of sales, net income, and cash flow, despite the fact that the 2008 downturn was much more severe.

In some parts of the world, policy makers encourage shorter hours as an alternative to layoffs. Many countries and more than half the states in the U.S. have some sort of "short-time" compensation program, whereby workers whose hours are reduced receive partial unemployment compensation. In France, 4% of workers and 1% of firms took advantage of short-time work programs in 2009, and the program paid off for both workers and companies. In a 2018 discussion paper for the European think tank Centre for Economic Policy Research, Pierre Cahuc, Francis Kramarz, and Sandra Nevoux found that companies that took advantage of the short-time work program laid off fewer workers and were more likely to survive during the Great Recession. The effect was most significant among the companies most severely hit by the recession and those with the highest levels of debt. According to the researchers, the short-time work approach allowed vulnerable companies to hold on to more of their workforce. Absent the subsidies, they most likely would have had to lay off more employees, making it more difficult to recover after the recession or causing them to go out of business altogether. The researchers estimate that for every five workers on short-time work, one job was saved. And they estimate that the cost per job saved was less than that of comparable programs; since the alternative was paying unemployment, the program actually saved the French government money.

One appealing thing about both furloughs and short-time work is that, as with layoffs, companies have discretion over which workers are affected. By contrast, across-the-board pay cuts or hiring freezes that fail to consider employee productivity can backfire, damaging morale and driving away the most productive employees. Similarly, hiring freezes affect every department indiscriminately, without weighing the value of various potential hires.

Performance pay—compensation based on some measure of productivity or business outcome—is another way to control labor costs without hurting productivity. There is a long-running debate about performance pay, for executives and frontline workers, and plenty of evidence for and against the management tool on both sides. But a recent study by Christos Makridis (of the White House Council of Economic Advisers) and Maury Gittleman (of the U.S. Bureau of Labor Statistics) documents an important fact. Using responses to the National Compensation Survey from 2004 to 2014, the study shows that U.S. companies rely on performance pay more frequently during economic downturns. Although they can't say whether this strategy works out for companies, they show that a given job is more likely to come with performance pay when times are tough. They hypothesize that this is because performance pay makes companies more flexible by aligning workers' incentives with changing conditions.

Invest in Technology

It's tempting to think of a recession as a time to batten down the hatches and play it safe. However, downturns actually appear to encourage the adoption of new technologies. In a 2018 paper, Brad Hershbein (of the Upjohn Institute for Employment Research) and Lisa B. Kahn (of the University of Rochester) compared more than 100 million online job listings posted from 2007 to 2015 with economic data to see how the Great Recession affected the types of skills employers were looking for. They found that the U.S. cities hardest hit by the recession saw a greater demand for higher-order skills—including computer-related skills. The boost in demand was partly due to employers' taking advantage of high unemployment to be choosier, as suggested by Alicia Sasser Modestino (of Northeastern), Daniel Shoag (of Harvard Kennedy School and Case Western Reserve), and Joshua Ballance (of the New England Public Policy

Center). Their study found that the demand for tech skills returns to more normal levels once the labor market improves.

But companies weren't only being choosier, Hershbein and Kahn found; they were becoming more digital, too. In those hard-hit areas of the United States, companies also increased their investment in information technology, driving the surge in IT skill requirements in their job postings.

Why do companies invest in technology during a recession when money is tight? Economists theorize that it's because their opportunity cost is lower than it would be in good times. When the economy is in great shape, a company has every incentive to produce as much as it can; if it diverts resources to invest in new technologies, it may be leaving money on the table. But when fewer people are willing to buy what you're selling, operations need not be kept humming at maximum capacity, which frees up operating budget to fund IT initiatives without dampening sales. For that reason, adopting technology costs less, in a sense, during a recession.

That's fine in theory, but other reasons may make more practical sense to managers. Technology can make your business more transparent, more flexible, and more efficient. According to Katy George, a senior partner at McKinsey, the first reason to prioritize digital transformation ahead of or during a downturn is that improved analytics can help management better understand the business, how the recession is affecting it, and where there's potential for operational improvements.

The second reason is that digital technology can help cut costs. Companies should prioritize "self-funding" transformation projects that pay off quickly, George says, such as automating tasks or adopting data-driven decision making. The third reason is that IT investments make companies more agile and therefore better able to handle the uncertainty and rapid change that come with a recession. In manufacturing, "we are finally seeing uptake now in the adoption of digital and advanced analytics," she says. It used to be that a manufacturer could be the cheapest in the market or could stay nimble—but not both. Flexibility came with serious costs. However, digital technologies "create much more flexibility around product changes, volume changes, etc., as well as around movement of your supply chain around the world."

That, in George's view, is one way the next recession might be different from past ones. Companies that have already made an investment in digital technology, analytics, and agile business practices may be better able to understand the threat they face and respond more quickly. As we've seen, recessions can create wide and long-standing performance gaps between companies. Research has found that digital technology can do the same. Companies that have neglected digital transformation may find that the next recession makes those gaps insurmountable.

Originally published in May–June 2019. Reprint R1903F

How to Bounce Back from Adversity

by Joshua D. Margolis and Paul G. Stoltz

THINGS ARE HUMMING ALONG, and then: A top client calls and says, "We're switching suppliers, starting next month. I'm afraid your company no longer figures into our plans." Or three colleagues, all of whom joined the organization around the same time you did, are up for promotion—but you aren't. Or your team loses another good person in a third round of layoffs; weak markets or no, you still need to make your numbers, but now you'll have to rely heavily on two of the most uncooperative members of the group.

So how do you react? Are you angry and disappointed, ranting and raving to anyone who will listen? Do you feel dejected and victimized, resigned to the situation even as you deny the cold reality of it? Or do you experience a rush of excitement—perhaps tinged with fear—because you sense an opportunity to develop your skills and talents in ways you'd never imagined? The truth is, you've probably reacted in all those ways when confronted with a challenge—maybe even cycling through multiple emotional states in the course of dealing with one really big mess.

Whatever your initial reaction, however, the challenge is to turn a negative experience into a productive one—that is, to counter adversity with resilience. Psychological resilience is the capacity to respond quickly and constructively to crises. It's a central dynamic in most survival stories, such as those of the shell-shocked individuals and organizations that rallied in the wake of 9/11 and Hurricane

Katrina. But resilience can be hard to muster for many reasons: Fear, anger, and confusion can paralyze us after a severe setback. Assigning blame rather than generating solutions is an all-too-human tendency. Worse yet, those to whom we turn for counsel may offer us exactly the wrong kind of advice.

Decades of research in psychology, on topics including hardiness, learned helplessness, coping, and the correlation between cognitive style and health, confirms that each of us has a distinct, consistent pattern of thinking about life's twists and turns—a pattern of which most of us are largely unaware. It may be an unconscious reflex to look backward from traumatic incidents to explain what just happened. Such analysis can be useful, certainly—but only up to the point where strong negative emotions start to prevent our moving on.

We believe that managers can build high levels of resilience in themselves and their teams by taking charge of how they think about adversity. Resilient managers move quickly from analysis to a plan of action (and reaction). After the onset of adversity, they shift from cause-oriented thinking to response-oriented thinking, and their focus is strictly forward. In our work with leaders in a variety of companies and industries, we've identified four lenses through which managers can view adverse events to make this shift effectively.

- **Control.** When a crisis hits, do you look for what you can improve now rather than trying to identify all the factors—even those beyond your control—that caused it in the first place?

- **Impact.** Can you sidestep the temptation to find the origins of the problem in yourself or others and focus instead on identifying what positive effects your personal actions might have?

- **Breadth.** Do you assume that the underlying cause of the crisis is specific and can be contained, or do you worry that it might cast a long shadow over all aspects of your life?

- **Duration.** How long do you believe that the crisis and its repercussions will last?

Idea in Brief

Psychological resilience—the capacity to respond quickly and constructively in a crisis—can be hard to muster when a manager is paralyzed by fear, anger, confusion, or a tendency to assign blame.

Resilient managers shift quickly from endlessly dissecting traumatic events to looking forward, determining the best course of action given new realities. They understand the size and scope of the crisis and the levels of control and impact they may have in a bad situation.

The authors describe a resilience regimen—a series of pointed questions designed to help managers replace negative responses with creative, resourceful ones and to move forward despite real or perceived obstacles.

The first two lenses characterize an individual's personal reaction to adversity, and the second two capture his or her impressions of the adversity's magnitude. Managers should consider all four to fully understand their instinctive responses to personal and professional challenges, setbacks, or failures.

In the following pages we'll describe a deliberative rather than reflexive approach to dealing with hardship—what we call a *resilience regimen*. By asking a series of pointed questions, managers can grasp their own and their direct reports' habits of thought and help reframe negative events in productive ways. With the four lenses as a guide, they can learn to stop feeling paralyzed by crisis, respond with strength and creativity, and help their direct reports do the same.

When Adversity Strikes

Most of us go with our gut when something bad happens. Deeply ingrained habits and beliefs sap our energy and keep us from acting constructively. People commonly fall into one of two emotional traps. One is *deflation*. Someone who has marched steadily through a string of successes can easily come to feel like a hero, able to fix any problem single-handedly. A traumatic event can snap that person back to reality. Even for the less heroic among us, adversity can touch off intense bursts of negative emotion—as if a dark cloud had settled behind our eyes, as one manager described it. We may feel disappointed in ourselves or others, mistreated and dispirited, even besieged.

That was the case with an executive we'll call Andrea, who headed up a major subsidiary of a U.S. automotive parts supplier. She had put up with years of internal bickering and the company's calcified cost structure. But over time she managed to bring the warring factions—unions, management, engineers, and marketers—together, and she gained widespread approval for a plan that would phase out old facilities and reduce crippling costs: Rather than try to supply every make and manufacturer, the company would focus on the truck market. Even more important, Andrea rallied everyone around a new line of products and a clear value proposition for customers that would rejuvenate the company's brand. The future looked bright.

Then fuel prices skyrocketed, the economy seized up, and demand from all segments of the truck market evaporated almost overnight. The recession had brought unfathomable challenges to the organization, and their suddenness left Andrea feeling as if she'd been socked in the stomach. After all her hard work, difficult conversations, and strategizing to fix the previous problems, she felt overmatched—for the first time in her career. Andrea lacked resilience precisely because she had a long history of wins.

The other emotional trap is *victimization*. Many of us assume the role of helpless bystander in the face of an adverse event. "Those people" have put us in an unfortunate position, we tell ourselves (and others) again and again. We dismiss both criticism and helpful suggestions from others, and go out of our way to affirm that we're right, everyone else is wrong, and no one understands us. Meanwhile, self-doubt may creep in, making us feel hopelessly constrained by circumstances.

Greg, a senior business development manager at an electronic accessories company, felt just this way. He had sailed through his first three years at the company with several promotions, taking on increasing responsibility—first for building brand awareness

among younger consumers, and then for building new relationships (and gaining more shelf space) with large retailers throughout
the United States and Canada. But as global competition heated up,
Greg's peers and superiors asked him to rethink his approach and
questioned whether retail outlets were still a viable distribution
channel. Big-box stores were squeezing the company's margins,
and physically servicing all the company's accounts seemed unnecessarily expensive compared with online options. Greg reacted to
his colleagues' requests by becoming more and more defensive and
extremely angry.

These stories illustrate the two-headed hydra of contemporary
adversity. First, highly accomplished managers are confronting, in
rapid succession, challenges the likes of which they've never seen
before—a worldwide economic crisis, the globalization of business,
the rise of new technologies, deep demographic shifts. Feeling dis-
couraged and helpless, they turn away from the problem and, unfortunately, from people who might be able to help. Second, even if
these managers went to their bosses for guidance, they'd most likely
receive inadequate coaching. That's because most supervisors, riding their own long wave of hard-won successes, lack the empathy
to intervene effectively. They may not know how to counsel direct
reports they feel aren't quite as talented as they were at escaping
the shadow of defeat. They may be so well accustomed to handling
adversity in ways that minimize their psychological stress that they
don't recognize their own bad habits. (See the sidebar "Coaching
Resilience.")

The Capacity for Resilience

Independent studies in psychology and our own observations suggest that the ability to bounce back from adversity hinges on uncov-
ering and untangling one's implicit beliefs about it—and shifting
how one responds.

Most of us, when we experience a difficult episode, make quick
assumptions about its causes, magnitude, consequences, and duration. We instantly decide, for example, whether it was inevitable,

Coaching Resilience

OFTEN EVEN THE MOST RESILIENT managers run into trouble trying to coach direct reports in crisis. They react with either a how-to pep talk delivered utterly without empathy or understanding, or a sympathetic ear and reassurance that things will turn out OK. Neither response will equip your team members to handle the next unforeseen twist or turn. Instead, you should adopt a collaborative, inquisitive approach that can help your direct reports generate their own options and possibilities.

Suppose a defensive employee were self-aware enough to ask you, his mentor, for help dealing with a professional setback—say, being passed over for promotion. You could just acknowledge his feelings and basically manage his response for him—outlining who he needs to talk to and in what order, and what to do if he doesn't get the answers he wants. But if you ask specifying, visualizing, and collaborating questions—such as "How can you step up to make the most immediate, positive impact on this situation?" and "How do you think your efforts in that direction would affect your team and your peers?"—you put the ball back in your employee's court. You're not endorsing any particular perspective, you're not providing absolute answers—you're helping to build resilience in a team member.

---

a function of forces beyond our control, or whether we could somehow have prevented it. Managers need to shift from this kind of reflexive thinking to "active" thinking about how best to respond, asking themselves what aspects they can control, what impact they can have, and how the breadth and duration of the crisis might be contained. Three types of questions can help them make this shift.

Specifying questions help managers identify ways to intervene; the more specific the answers, the better. *Visualizing questions* help shift their attention away from the adverse event and toward a more positive outcome. *Collaborating questions* push them to reach out to others—not for affirmation or commiseration but for joint problem solving. Each type of question can clarify each of the four lenses of resilient thinking.

Taken together, the four sets make up the resilience regimen. Let's take a closer look at each set in turn.

Control

According to multiple studies—including those by Bernard Weiner, of UCLA, and James Amirkhan, of Cal State Long Beach, and the classic University of Chicago study of executives by Suzanne Ouellette and Salvatore Maddi—our reactions to stressful situations depend on the degree of control we believe we can exercise. Andrea struggled with whether she could still contribute meaningfully to her company or whether the sudden shifts in the economy had moved the situation beyond her control. If Greg continued to attribute criticism of his retail strategy to "scheming peers," he might fail to see what he personally could do to influence the company's long-term strategy or his own destiny. The following questions can help managers identify ways to exercise control over what happens next:

Specifying: What aspects of the situation can I directly influence to change the course of this adverse event?

Visualizing: What would the manager I most admire do in this situation?

Collaborating: Who on my team can help me, and what's the best way to engage that person or those people?

The goal in asking these questions is not to come up with a final plan of action or an immediate understanding of how the team should react. Rather, it is to generate possibilities—to develop, in a disciplined and concrete way, an inventory of what *might* be done. (The next set of questions can help managers outline what *will* be done.) Had Andrea asked herself these three questions, she might have identified an opportunity to, say, rally the company around emerging safety and fuel-efficiency devices in the industry, or to use the slowdown to perfect the company's newer, still-promising products by working more closely with major customers. Similarly, if Greg had undertaken the exercise, he might have been able to channel something his mentor once told him: "It's not about whether I'm right or wrong. It's about what's best for the company." With that in mind, Greg might have clearly seen the benefits of reaching out to his peers and team members to assess alternative go-to-market approaches.

The Research Behind the Resilience Regimen

TWO CONVERGING STREAMS OF RESEARCH informed our work. The first examines how patterns of understanding the world shape people's responses to stressful situations. Albert Ellis and Aaron Beck pioneered this research, followed by, among others, Martin Seligman and Christopher Peterson on learned helplessness; Richard Lazarus and Susan Folkman on coping; and Lyn Abramson, David Burns, and James Amirkhan on how "attributional styles" affect health. More recently, Karen Reivich and Andrew Shatté identified how people can strengthen their resilience.

The second stream, pioneered by Suzanne Ouellette and Salvatore Maddi in their studies of hardiness and extended most recently by Deborah Khoshaba and Aaron Antonovsky, explored what differentiated two groups of people who encountered intense stress. One group flourished while the other sank.

A common finding emerges from these two streams of inquiry: How people approach trying circumstances influences both their ability to deal with them and, ultimately, their own success and well-being.

The ingenuity and work ethic he had applied to building the retail business could have been turned to devising the next great strategy.

Impact
Related to our beliefs about whether we can turn things around are our assumptions about what caused a negative event: Did the problem originate with us personally, or somewhere else? Greg attributed the criticism of his retail distribution strategy to his "competitive, power-hungry" colleagues rather than to the possible shortcomings of his approach. He was too deeply mired in defensiveness to get out of his own way. Andrea felt powerless in the face of challenges she'd never before had to meet and forces that eclipsed her individual initiative and effort. Instead of giving in to deflation and victimization, managers can focus intently on how they might affect the event's outcome.

Specifying: How can I step up to make the most immediate, positive impact on this situation?

Visualizing: What positive effect might my efforts have on those around me?

Collaborating: How can I mobilize the efforts of those who are hanging back?

If he had focused on these questions, Greg might have seen that he was not simply being asked to discard his accounts and acknowledge that his strategy was misguided; rather, he was being cast as a potential player in the organization's change efforts. He might have appreciated that openly and rigorously assessing his business-development strategy could influence others—whether his assessment validated the status quo or led to a solution no one had thought of yet. And he might have reignited the entrepreneurial culture he so valued when he joined the company by soliciting others' input on the marketing strategy. For her part, Andrea knew all too well that her company's fortunes depended on economic conditions—but she couldn't see how her response to the market failures might energize the organization. These questions might have helped her.

Breadth

When we encounter a setback, we tend to assume that its causes are either specific to the situation or more broadly applicable, like poison that will taint everything we touch. To build up resilience, managers need to stop worrying about the reach of the causes and focus instead on how to limit the damage. These questions may even highlight opportunities in the midst of chaos.

Specifying: What can I do to reduce the potential downside of this adverse event—by even 10%? What can I do to maximize the potential upside—by even 10%?

Visualizing: What strengths and resources will my team and I develop by addressing this event?

Collaborating: What can each of us do on our own, and what can we do collectively, to contain the damage and transform the situation into an opportunity?

These questions might have helped Andrea achieve two core objectives. Instead of endlessly revisiting the repercussions of plummeting truck sales, she might have identified large and small ways in which she and her team could use the economic crisis to reconfigure the company's manufacturing processes. And rather than fixating on how awful and extensive the damage to the organization was, she could have imagined a new postrecession norm—thriving in the face of tighter resources, more selective customers, and more exacting government scrutiny. Greg might have seen that he had a rare opportunity to gain valuable leadership skills and relevant insights about competitors' marketing strategies by engaging peers and team members in reassessing the retail strategy.

Duration

Some hardships in the workplace seem to have no end in sight—underperformance quarter after quarter, recurring clashes between people at different levels and in different parts of the company, a stalled economy. But questions about duration can put the brakes on such runaway nightmares. Here, though, it's important to begin by imagining the desired outcome.

A change in mindset

Cause-oriented thinking	Response-oriented thinking
Control Was this adverse event inevitable, or could I have prevented it?	What features of the situation can I (even potentially) improve?
Impact Did I cause the adverse event, or did it result from external forces?	What sort of positive impact can I personally have on what happens next?
Breadth Is the underlying cause of this event specific to it or more widespread?	How can I contain the negatives of this situation and generate currently unseen positives?
Duration Is the underlying cause of this event enduring or temporary?	What can I do to begin addressing the problem now?

Visualizing: What do I want life to look like on the other side of this adversity?

Specifying: What can I do in the next few minutes, or hours, to move in that direction?

Collaborating: What sequence of steps can we put together as a team, and what processes can we develop and adopt, to see us through to the other side of this hardship?

Greg was sure that criticism of his business-development approach signaled the end: no more promotions, no more recognition from higher-ups of his hard work and tangible results, nothing to look forward to but doing others' bidding in a company that was sowing the seeds of decline. These three questions might have broadened his outlook. That is, he might have seen the benefits of quickly arranging meetings with his mentor (for personal counsel) and with his team (for professional input on strategy). The questions could have been a catalyst for listing the data required to make a case for or against change, the analyses the team would need to run, and the questions about various sales channels and approaches that needed to be answered. This exercise might have helped Greg see a workable path through the challenge he was experiencing. The result would have been renewed confidence that he and his team could keep their company at the forefront of customer service.

Answering the Questions

Although the question sets offer a useful framework for retraining managers' responses, simply knowing what to ask isn't enough. You won't become more resilient simply because you've read this far and have made a mental note to pull out these questions the next time a destabilizing difficulty strikes. To strengthen your capacity for resilience, you need to internalize the questions by following two simple precepts:

Write down the answers. Various studies on stress and coping with trauma demonstrate that the act of writing about difficult episodes can enhance an individual's emotional and physical well-being. Indeed, writing offers people command over an adverse situation in a way that merely thinking about it does not. It's best to treat the resilience regimen as a timed exercise: Give yourself at least 15 minutes, uninterrupted, to write down your responses to the 12 questions. That may seem both too long and too short—too long because managers rarely have that much time for any activity, let alone one involving personal reflection. But you'll actually end up saving time. Instead of ruminating about events, letting them interrupt your work, you'll have solutions in the making. As you come to appreciate and rely on this exercise, 15 minutes may feel too short.

Do it every day. When you're learning any new skill, repetition is critical. The resilience regimen is a long-term fitness plan, not a crash diet. You must ask and answer these questions daily if they are to become second nature. But that can't happen if bad habits crowd out the questions. You don't need to experience a major trauma to practice; you can ask yourself the questions in response to daily annoyances that sap your energy—a delayed flight, a slow computer, an unresponsive colleague. You can use the four lenses in virtually any order, but it's important to start with your weakest dimension. If you tend to blame others and overlook your own potential to contribute, start with the impact questions. If you tend to worry that the adverse event will ruin everything, start with the breadth questions.

Under ongoing duress, executives' capacity for resilience is critical to maintaining their mental and physical health. Paradoxically, however, building resilience is best done precisely when times are most difficult—when we face the most upending challenges, when we are at the greatest risk of misfiring with our reactions, when we are blindest to the opportunities presented. All the more reason, then, to use the resilience regimen to tamp down unproductive responses to adversity, replace negativity with creativity and resourcefulness, and get things done despite real or perceived obstacles.

Originally published in January–February 2010. Reprint R1001E

Rohm and Haas's Former CEO on Pulling Off a Sweet Deal in a Down Market

by Raj Gupta

SHORTLY BEFORE CHRISTMAS 2008, I left my office at the specialty chemicals company Rohm and Haas for what I thought would be the last time. I had spent much of the year leading up to my long-planned retirement orchestrating the sale of the company—a deal with its former rival Dow Chemical had been forged in July 2008—and there was little left to do but hand over the reins. I had succeeded at one of the hardest goals I'd ever been set: quietly negotiating a friendly sale for $18 billion. All we still needed was the Federal Trade Commission approval that, per our agreement, would trigger the close of the deal within 48 hours. As I drove away from the office on December 18, a colleague called to say that, as planned, my office had been essentially demolished in preparation for its new occupant. My assistant had been reassigned to work with our COO. My work with Rohm and Haas was finished.

But it nagged at me that I hadn't heard recently from Andrew Liveris, Dow's chairman and CEO. Market conditions had worsened globally, and the equity and credit markets were in turmoil. Dow had been expecting a large cash influx of $9.5 billion from a proposed joint venture with Kuwait Petroleum. On December 29 Kuwait canceled the venture. But our deal with Dow was unconditional. And then I got the call.

"Raj, you and I need to sit down and go over where we are," Liveris said. Because I didn't even have an office at Rohm and Haas anymore, I had to arrange for temporary space at our Philadelphia headquarters—and a temporary assistant. When we met, I learned that Dow saw no way to get the cash it needed elsewhere, given the state of the financial markets and its own deteriorating financial performance.

I organized an emergency conference call to brief the directors on the situation. We believed that our contract with Dow was airtight. Our shareholders had approved the transaction in October by an overwhelming majority. The board and I had a fiduciary responsibility to complete the deal.

I had led the process from the beginning, and the board was very clear that it was my role to see it to an end—one way or another. My personal credibility was on the line.

An Unexpected Request

In November 2007, representatives of the Haas family trusts, which collectively owned 32% of outstanding shares, had asked me to explore disposing of all or most of their holdings at a "full and fair" price within 12 to 18 months. The timing and nature of the request were surprising. Until then the trusts had appeared to be very happy with the level of their ownership and the performance of the company. The board and I, perhaps naively, believed that as long as John C. Haas, the 89-year-old son of the founder, was alive, no such request would be made. We clearly did not read the tea leaves.

Rohm and Haas had been a quiet but steady business since its founding, in 1909. Our performance had been strong, with an average annual return to shareholders of 13.5% since 1949. For the past 30 years we had increased our dividends by an average of 10% a year. The majority of shares were held by the family trusts, several large

Idea in Brief

Raj Gupta had led the specialty chemical company Rohm and Haas without drama for years when some of its most important shareholders asked him to orchestrate its sale. Surprised but determined to do his best for the company, in July 2008 he arranged an $18 billion deal with competitor Dow Chemical, which the industry press called the "deal of the century."

But Dow was relying on cash from a planned joint venture of its own with Kuwait Petroleum, and when the stock market plummeted, the joint venture—and

Dow's financing—fell through. Then things got really interesting. Would Dow try to walk away from the deal? Could Rohm and Haas insist that it go through in spite of the unforeseen global meltdown? How airtight was that agreement? Gupta, who learned he had cancer in the midst of all this, had to find a way through the complicated financial and economic issues. In this first-person account he talks about the most difficult deliverable ever asked of him—seeing through the sale of his company as the world economy was collapsing.

institutional shareholders, and employees. I was only the sixth CEO in the company's history. In my 10 years as CEO, the board hadn't faced any big, difficult decisions until now.

I took my leadership in the sale very personally, and I was determined to keep the company whole and operating smoothly during this extended period of uncertainty. I spent months exploring options and strategies with the board and our outside advisers. In hindsight, the timing couldn't have been worse. The economy was starting to weaken, and the request that we sell for all cash at a premium price, though entirely reasonable, limited our options. We identified just three companies as strategic buyers—on the basis of their interest, their ability to finance a transaction of this size, and the likely business synergies: BASF, with headquarters in Germany; Dow, based in Michigan; and DuPont, based in Delaware.

I had layers of concern: What if potential buyers didn't show up? What if our discreet outreach to potential buyers was inconclusive, just as the economy was rapidly deteriorating? The worst possible outcome, I thought, would be an aborted process; our key stakeholders would doubt our strategy and future at a time when we needed steady support and performance.

Rohm and Haas's success rested on building relations for the medium to long term. Our position was downstream in the industry value chain; our customers relied on the performance embedded in our science and our commitment to ongoing technology support. Confidence in our future was essential. A mishandled disclosure or rumormongering would cause chaos among our employees and customers and risk destroying the foundations of the enterprise.

I had invested a great deal of time and effort in forming personal relationships with many of my peers—in particular the CEOs of BASF, Dow, and DuPont. The burden was on me to deliver a buyer, so I arranged individual face-to-face meetings with them to plant the seed. I told them we recognized that financial conditions were not as favorable as they could be, but our board supported my outreach. If they wanted to explore this opportunity, they'd have to get back to me swiftly.

The Brewing Deal

Within a week Andrew Liveris called to say he was ready to talk. He came to Philadelphia with an all-cash bid of $74 a share—in the range of value our advisers had suggested. At that time our stock was trading at $52 a share, and the highest it had ever gone was $62. His offer was good for only 48 hours.

The board concluded that it was our fiduciary duty to get in touch with BASF and DuPont to see if they wanted to make an offer. BASF's CEO, Jürgen Hambrecht, returned my call within 15 minutes. "Raj," he said, "I was hoping you were calling me to say that this whole process is off, given what's going on in the world." But he promised to get back to me quickly, and he did—with an offer of $70 a share, all cash, no conditions except regulatory approval. DuPont, however, let us know that its interest was restricted to only part of our portfolio.

The brewing deal was so secret that I virtually lived a double life for months. Only the board, six people within the company, and a few of our outside advisers knew about it. I was the focal point for all information and decisions. All our meetings were held offsite and during off hours, including many weekends.

We announced the deal with Dow on July 10—at a final price of $78 a share—and I'm sure that every Rohm and Haas employee in the world was in absolute shock. The shareholders were delighted, however, and the industry press called it the "deal of the century." From July into the fall, the stress of seeing the deal through took its toll on me. We worked hard to keep employees, shareholders, and customers well informed and comfortable about the company's future. But I was getting e-mails at midnight: "Are you awake?" The answer was always yes, I'm awake. There were 22 board meetings and dozens of phone calls with the directors from the time we first explored the idea of selling the company until the deal closed. I knew it was crucial that I present a calm face to my staff, but I was constantly worried.

In August, totally unexpectedly, I learned that I had prostate cancer, which added a new dimension to my stress. A low point came when I passed out on a flight to Germany and had to be admitted for emergency care. I withdrew from day-to-day operations to focus on my health and had surgery a few months later. My sole responsibility to the company remained seeing the deal through.

When Liveris and I met in January 2009, it was with just one key adviser each. He laid out all his concerns and issues and what he was trying to resolve. I could see that he had a Herculean task on his hands. "Andrew," I said, "I understand what you're dealing with, but you have to put yourself in my situation. I need something to take to my board. I'd like to tell them that you fully intend to close the deal but you need more time. Give me a deadline, and we can go public with an announcement that this is the situation." I offered to assist with the Haas family trusts to get some kind of bridge financing. Liveris didn't want to pursue that. Ultimately, he offered to let us know by June whether Dow could do the deal or not.

On January 23 we got FTC approval for the deal. According to the contract, Dow had just two working days to close the transaction. That was simply not going to happen. Dow's backup financing lines

Timeline of the deal: July 10, 2008, to April 1, 2009

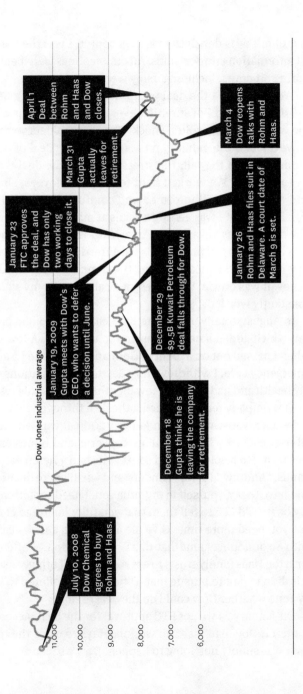

Dow Jones industrial average

July 10, 2008
Dow Chemical agrees to buy Rohm and Haas.

December 18
Gupta thinks he is leaving the company for retirement.

December 29
$9.5B Kuwait Petroleum deal falls through for Dow.

January 19, 2009
Gupta meets with Dow's CEO, who wants to defer a decision until June.

January 23
FTC approves the deal, and Dow has only two working days to close it.

January 26
Rohm and Haas files suit in Delaware. A court date of March 9 is set.

March 4
Dow reopens talks with Rohm and Haas.

March 31
Gupta actually leaves for retirement.

April 1
Deal between Rohm and Haas and Dow closes.

11,000

10,000

9,000

8,000

7,000

6,000

would expire in June, but I believed that the company had enough resources, given time, to complete the deal under the original terms. Nevertheless, we had to protect our shareholders. With the board's approval, we filed suit in Delaware, asking the court for an expedited hearing to enforce our contract. Everyone was well aware of the significance of that lawsuit: We were essentially asking the court to decide whether Dow—and implicitly any other company—should be held to the terms of a deal regardless of external conditions. Our court date was set for March 9, and we knew the world would be watching.

Our board sent a letter, which we made public, to Dow's board, urging it to take control of the situation and honor the contract. Speculation in the financial press was intense: Would the transaction close? If it didn't, would our share price fall dramatically? Would Dow be forced into bankruptcy or have to sell valuable assets to close the deal?

I spent this period explaining to Rohm and Haas employees why we had to take this drastic action and why it was in their best interests and our customers' that the deal go through. My energy went into urging employees to stay calm, keeping the board informed, and communicating with key customers, the Haas family trusts, and our large hedge fund shareholders.

On Wednesday, March 4, less than a week before we were set to square off in court, I received an e-mail from Andrew Liveris. "Raj," he wrote, "should we give this one last try?" We agreed to meet in New York the next day, along with our respective advisers. We also decided that each of us would bring one highly respected board member to help facilitate the process. Our discussion focused on two key points: how to obtain bridge equity sufficient to reduce the debt financing required and how to keep Dow's credit rating from being downgraded to junk status by Standard & Poor's and Moody's.

Dow came up with some creative solutions, including working out arrangements with two of Rohm and Haas's largest shareholders, the Haas family trusts and Paulson & Co., to obtain the equity financing. And we participated in calls with S&P and Moody's to persuade them that Dow's situation warranted "investment grade"

How Did the Deal Work Out for Dow?

by Karen Dillon

ON JULY 10, 2008, when the deal with Rohm and Haas was announced, Dow's share price was around $35. The following March, as Dow scrambled to find alternatives to a collapsed joint venture with Kuwait Petroleum, it dipped to an interday low of under $6.

Ultimately, Dow arranged a bridge loan of more than $9 billion, sold a $3 billion equity stake to Rohm and Haas's two major shareholders, and procured investments of $3 billion from Berkshire Hathaway and $1 billion from the Kuwait Investment Authority.

The market waited to see if that complex financing would crush Dow under its weight. But Dow paid off the bridge loan ahead of schedule, retired the debt to purchase Rohm and Haas, and has made a profit in every quarter since. The acquisition "was a pivotal point in the transformation of Dow," says a company spokesperson. Dow's so-called performance businesses, which include the majority of former Rohm and Haas assets, accounted for nearly two-thirds of its sales in the second quarter of 2010. By mid-September the company's shares hovered near $26.

The relationship between the two CEOs survived the ordeal as well. "A week after the closing [Dow CEO Andrew Liveris] sent me a case of excellent Australian wine as a thank-you," Gupta says. "And we continue to maintain cordial relations."

---

status. This was all hastily done in the days before our Monday court appointment. At 8 p.m. on Sunday, Andrew called me and said, "Raj, we're making progress. We don't have all the answers yet, but can you go to the judge and tell him that we are working on it?" In court the next morning we asked the judge for more time, and he said, "You can have all the time you want." I think he was relieved.

By 4 p.m. that day Dow had arranged its financing and we had an agreement, which we asked the judge to read into the record. The same day—one of the lowest points of the year for the stock market—Dow's directors signed off on the deal. Up until then I hadn't been certain it would really happen. Our stock had been trading down, and at one point it went under $50 a share. But in the end we got the $18 billion.

On March 31, I finally left Rohm and Haas for the last time. The deal closed the following day. I hadn't allowed myself to breathe a sigh of relief until that moment. It was a bittersweet victory for me, because I had invested so much of my time and energy in building the organization and managing for the long term that it was hard to let it go. I took solace in the fact that most of the family trusts' proceeds from the sale were invested in charities right away. There's a sense, though, that the company doesn't exist anymore, which is sad for me.

But I concluded that I could move on with my life—the retirement I had long planned. I'm not certain I could lucidly recite that day's events. Certainly I can't offer profound reflections on them. At the time, I was focused on the misfortune of having had to deal with this problem at the end of my career. Now, with the benefit of more than a year's hindsight, I recognize that we had a strong dose of good fortune, too, which allowed us to achieve this nearly impossible outcome.

Originally published in November 2010. Reprint R1011A

How to Be a Good Boss in a Bad Economy

by Robert I. Sutton

THESE ARE TOUGH TIMES for every boss I know. Fear and paranoia are running wild, not just in financial markets but in workplaces, too. A few weeks back a weary executive at a professional services firm told me how painful it had been to lay off 10% of his people and how he was struggling to comfort and inspire those who remained. When I asked a mutual friend, the CEO of a manufacturing firm, to "show some love" to this distressed executive, he jumped in to help—but admitted that he was wrestling with his own demons, having just implemented a 20% workforce reduction.

It was not a coincidence to find two friends in such similar straits; few organizations seem to have avoided them. Even in businesses renowned for having heart, bosses have been forced to wield the ax. NetApp, declared number one in *Fortune*'s "100 Best Companies to Work For" for 2009, announced it was cutting loose 6% of its employees less than a month after the ranking appeared. Google, top-rated by *Fortune* in 2008, has shed hundreds of full-time employees. And layoffs aren't the only reason it's a miserable time to be the boss. Where cuts haven't occurred, people suspect they will, and the lingering dread creates its own challenges. One technology sector CEO I've worked with for years felt compelled to inform his people in writing that not only were no layoffs planned but the company would be hiring a lot more people in the coming year. Yet, he said, "no matter how much I share about how safe we are, people still ask, When are the layoffs coming?" Even where jobs are demonstrably safe, lesser but real disappointments occur: Salaries are cut, budgets are pared, projects are back-burnered.

As a result, most bosses—like you, perhaps—are operating in difficult and sometimes unfamiliar territory. Equipped with skills and approaches honed over long years of business growth, they now find their roles defined by an unexpected question: How should people be managed when fear is in the air, confidence is slipping, and it looks as if the road ahead will remain rough for many miles? This isn't the job most executives and managers signed on for, and not everyone will rise to the occasion. This article is designed to help those who want to do so—first by clarifying why it's so hard to be a good boss, and then by sharing the essence of what the best bosses do during tough times.

The Toxic Tandem

Let's be clear: It's never easy to be a great boss, even in good economic times. It's challenging in part because of an unfortunate dynamic that naturally arises in relationships of unequal power. Research confirms what many of us have long suspected: People who gain authority over others tend to become more self-centered and less mindful of what others need, do, and say. That would be bad enough, but the problem is compounded because a boss's self-absorbed words and deeds are scrutinized so closely by his or her followers. Combined, these tendencies make for a toxic tandem that deserves closer study.

To appreciate the first half of the dynamic—that bosses tend to be oblivious to their followers' perspectives—consider the "cookie experiment" reported by the psychologists Dacher Keltner, Deborah H. Gruenfeld, and Cameron Anderson in 2003. In this study, teams of three students each were instructed to produce a short policy paper. Two members of each team were randomly assigned to

Idea in Brief

It's not easy being the boss during a downturn. Your natural impulse is to focus on your own well-justified concerns, but your people are watching your every move for clues to their fate.

You need to rethink your responsibilities in terms of what your people may lack most in unsettling times: predictability, understanding, control, and compassion.

By making tough times less traumatic, you'll equip your organization to thrive when conditions improve—and earn the loyalty of individuals who will remain in your network for years to come.

write the paper. The third member evaluated it and determined how much the other two would be paid, in effect making them subordinates. About 30 minutes into the meeting, the experimenter brought in a plate of five cookies—a welcome break that was in fact the focus of the experiment. No one was expected to reach for the last cookie on the plate, and no one did. Basic manners dictate such restraint. But what of the fourth cookie—the extra one that could be taken without negotiation or an awkward moment? It turns out that a little taste of power has a substantial effect. The "bosses" not only tended to take the fourth cookie but also displayed signs of "disinhibited" eating, chewing with their mouths open and scattering crumbs widely.

It's a cute little experiment, but it beautifully illustrates a finding consistent across many studies. When people—independent of personality—wield power, their ability to lord it over others causes them to (1) become more focused on their own needs and wants; (2) become less focused on others' needs, wants, and actions; and (3) act as if written and unwritten rules that others are expected to follow don't apply to them. To make matters worse, many bosses suffer a related form of power poisoning: They believe that they are aware of every important development in the organization (even when they are remarkably ignorant of key facts). This affliction is called "the fallacy of centrality"—the assumption that because one holds a central position, one automatically knows everything necessary to exercise effective leadership.

Idea in Practice

Some years ago Robert Sutton led a workshop with the senior managers of Procter & Gamble that touched on the importance of providing workers with predictability, understanding, control, and compassion. It turned out that his framework aligned with what they'd already learned in the context of plant closings. John E. Pepper, Jr., who was then P&G's chairman, explained an internal analysis of the effects that management's actions had on productivity, retention of employees who were offered jobs elsewhere in the company, and sales in the cities where the closings occurred. Plant closings did far less damage when leaders:

1. Announced the closing date and key milestones well in advance and described how events would unfold both for employees and for members of the affected community.

2. Explained in detail to employees and the community the business case for closing the plant.

3. Gave affected employees options for finding other jobs inside the company or resources to job hunt outside.

4. Expressed human concern—in public and in private—to affected employees and community officials.

In other words, P&G executives saw the value of predictability, understanding, control, and compassion in times of distressing organizational change.

Now let's look at the other half of the dynamic—that followers devote immense energy to watching, interpreting, and worrying about even the smallest and most innocent moves their superiors make. This is something we've long known about animals; studies of baboon troops show that the typical member glances at the alpha male every 20 or 30 seconds to see what he is doing. And although people don't check what their boss is doing two or three times a minute, this tendency is well documented in human groups, too. As the psychologist Susan Fiske puts it, "Attention is directed up the hierarchy. Secretaries know more about their bosses than vice versa; graduate students know more about their advisors than vice versa." Fiske explains: "People pay attention to those who control their outcomes. In an effort to predict and possibly influence what is going to happen to them, people gather information about those with power." Further, people tend to interpret what they see the boss do in a negative light. Keltner and his colleagues report that when the top dog makes an ambiguous move (one that isn't clearly good or bad for followers), followers are most likely to construe it as a sign that something bad is going to happen to them. Related studies also show that when people down the pecking order feel threatened by their superiors, they become distracted from their work. They redirect their efforts to trying to figure out what is going on and to coping with their fear and anxiety—perhaps searching the web for insight or huddling with their peers to gossip, complain, and exchange emotional support. As a result, performance suffers.

Even in the best of times, bosses fall prey to this toxic tandem. In a crisis, however, both sides of the dynamic are amplified. So it's not your imagination; it is harder to be a good boss in a bad economy. Your own stress presses you to shut down emotionally, to focus attention on what your superiors are up to, to turn inward and wrestle with your fears. The heightened threat causes your followers to watch your moves even more closely, searching for clues about what is likely to happen to them and what they can do about it. The threats that arise in tough times are also more likely to be real than imagined, and to hit with greater frequency. Everyone involved is only human, with the usual foibles, quirks, and blind spots. The equipment remains the same, and it's being put to an unusually hard test.

How can well-intentioned bosses avoid the toxic tandem? By mindfully taking attention from themselves in order to give it to their people's challenges and worries. Bosses who do so will find that in stressful times people have an acute—and often unmet— need for four remedies: predictability, understanding, control, and compassion. My mentor Robert Kahn and I outlined the first three in a 1987 paper that was inspired by the great and lousy bosses we had observed during a deep recession in the midwestern United States. Some years later my colleague Jeffrey Pfeffer helped me recognize the fourth as a distinct and equally crucial antidote to organizational stress.

Making the Best of a Bad Situation

WHETHER YOU OVERSEE JUST a few direct reports or are the CEO of a big company, these frightening times mean that you need to rethink your responsibilities as the boss. More than anything, people now need you to address deficits in four areas:

1. Predictability

Give people as much information as you can about what will happen and when. If shocks are preceded by fair warnings, people not only have time to brace themselves but also get chances to breathe easy.

2. Understanding

Explain why the changes you're implementing are necessary—and don't assume you need to do so only once.

3. Control

Take a bewildering challenge and break it down into "small win" opportunities. In situations where you can't give people much influence over what happens, at least give them a say in how it happens.

4. Compassion

Put yourself in the other person's shoes. Express empathy and—when appropriate—sorrow for any painful actions that have to be taken.

Providing Predictability

The importance of predictability in people's lives is hard to overstate, and has been demonstrated in numerous studies. The most famous is Martin Seligman's research on the signal/safety hypothesis. Seligman observed that when a stressful event can be predicted, the absence of a stressful event can also be predicted. Thus a person knows when he or she need not maintain a state of vigilance or anxiety. Seligman cites the function of air-raid sirens during the bombing of London in World War II. They were so reliable a signal that people felt free to go about their business when the sirens were silent. The hypothesis was bolstered by studies in which some animals and not others were given a warning in advance of a shock. Those that were never warned lived in a constant state of anxiety.

The same holds true for organizational shocks like layoffs. If you give people as much information as you can about what will happen (to them as individuals, to their work groups, and to the organization as a whole) and when it will happen, they will prepare to the extent they can and suffer less. Just as important, they can learn to relax in the absence of such a warning. This was the thinking behind one CEO's decision to issue a heads-up memo to the staff of his nonprofit organization. In it he laid out in detail the worst-case scenario that would result if the stock market and donations failed to rebound over a certain time period. But while preparing people for a future that might well involve job losses, he also made a firm commitment: No one would be asked to leave for at least three months. At another company I know, managers opted for a deeper staff cut than was immediately necessary, because they were determined not to inflict a second one right away and thus create a distracting fear of still more to come. They followed that cut with the message that although more might be needed in the future, none would be made for at least six months.

Providing more predictability is in large part a function of reducing the seemingly random. Certainly there are times when people seek out surprise and novelty. Most of us come to points in our lives when, in the words of Arthur Conan Doyle, we abhor the dull routine of existence. This is not one of them. It is also important to realize that what will be seen as surprising or routine, as fair or unfair, is dictated by the quirks of your organization's history. Unfortunately, the better you have treated your people in the past, the more bruised they will be by layoffs, pay cuts, and other blows. When Advanced Micro Devices, which once touted its no-layoffs policy and called other firms that used layoffs "myopic as well as misanthropic," had to resort to staff cuts in 1986, the resulting anger and despair struck many as disproportionate. The same intensity of reaction was seen when other historically humane companies—Levi Strauss and Hewlett-Packard come to mind—were forced to lay off employees. Meanwhile, companies with a history of treating people as mere expenses and tossing surplus bodies out the door at the first whiff of bad times seem scarcely to miss a beat. After all, that is what

Beware the Cone of Silence

FROM AN EMPLOYEE'S PERSPECTIVE, when to get nervous is often obvious: Bosses start huddling behind closed doors, deciding God knows what, and betraying as little as possible. As a boss, you might find some such "backstage work" unavoidable—but be aware that it can reinforce feelings of unpredictability, misunderstanding, lack of control, and management's indifference, which will ultimately make things harder on everyone.

Don't Hide

In the worst cases I've seen, bosses have even hidden from their people: Knowing what they knew about impending cost cutting, they couldn't look subordinates in the eye. Years ago, when colleagues and I studied the collapse of the video game company Atari, we learned that top executives were using a back door rather than the front entrance to come and go, so determined were they to avoid contact with the rank and file. That study came to mind when, quite recently, a boss I know disappeared from his office for weeks after a layoff. In each case employees interpreted leadership's absence as a sign that something truly horrible was going to happen. The rumor mill sped up, and even less effort went into the work at hand.

Be Discreet

To be sure, the answer cannot be that senior managers should spend less time conferring. In a downturn the pressure is immense to make decisions that demand a shared understanding of rapidly evolving financials, scenarios and options, and constraints. Often it is impossible to open up this messy decision process to broader involvement and scrutiny, which might not only threaten legal and ethical requirements for confidentiality but could lead

their people expect. A 2006 study of 3,080 Canadian workplaces by Christopher Zatzick and Roderick Iverson showed that layoffs had the most negative effect on productivity in "high involvement" organizations—places where employees have greater responsibility and decision-making authority, and where more emphasis is put on treating people well than in traditional workplaces. Zatzick and Iverson also found that productivity dropped most sharply in once-enlightened workplaces that had shattered employee expectations with a one-two punch: They did deep layoffs *and* abandoned high-involvement work practices. The effort that people are willing to expend and the anger and anxiety that they suffer don't simply to worse decisions. (As the psychologist Philip Tetlock has shown, decision makers operating under excessive scrutiny tend to make the choices that are easiest to justify rather than those they think are best.) Information leaks can also hurt people or be downright embarrassing. Witness the chagrin of a major law firm in February 2009 after one of its partners had a sensitive phone conversation with the firm's COO while riding on a train from Washington, DC, to New York. Fellow passengers could not help overhearing that the firm was planning deep staff cuts in March, and at least one person deduced what firm the partner was with after he rattled off the names of two dozen candidates for dismissal. That passenger promptly posted the news in a blog, and the story spread like wildfire. (To its credit, the firm quickly apologized for the indiscretion and acknowledged that the news was true.)

Rely on Your Peers

Some closed-door mystery is clearly inevitable. And even the hardiest of bosses need some time away from the fray to recharge. But don't let such absences go unexplained. Your employees can appreciate the stress you are under, and won't begrudge you an occasional break. You won't want to burden them with your troubles when they have their own—but you and your management team can support one another, and you'll be available to talk about the team's fears and problems along the way.

The key is to be deeply sensitive to people's interpretations. Follow long closed-door meetings with longer open-door periods. Communicate everything that can be communicated, both in writing and face-to-face. Be present and visibly on top of the situation. Express warmth and concern, but also whatever optimism is warranted. Above all, look your people in the eye.

result from their objective fate; their reactions are shaped by the difference between what they expect and what they get.

Increasing Understanding

If predictability is about what will happen and when, understanding is about why and how. The chief advice here is to accompany any major change with an explanation of what makes it necessary and what effect it will have—in as much detail as possible. This advice, too, is rooted in psychological research: Human beings consistently react negatively to unexplained events. The effect is so strong that it is better to give an explanation they dislike than no explanation at all, provided the explanation is credible.

Good bosses also know that more than a single communication is needed to bring a large group to a point of real understanding. I mentioned above the technology CEO whose people persisted in expecting job losses even though the business was growing. Rather than assuming that his "no layoffs" message would suffice until further notice, he knew he would have to keep repeating himself and looked for other ways to help employees comprehend the reality. "We shared our bank statements with everyone," he told me, "so that they could understand where our assets are and how safe they are."

When operations are going haywire and people are rattled, it's especially hard to get new ideas to take root or to teach new behaviors of any complexity. Your job as boss is to design messages that will get through to people who are distracted, upset, and apt to think negatively given any ambiguity. When it comes to internal communications, your mantra should be "Simple, concrete, and repetitive." Think of the attendants on Flight 1549, in what has been called the Miracle on the Hudson. As the plane plummeted down, they chanted in unison, "Brace, brace, heads down, stay down." Bosses who lead people through crises need to provide the same kind of clear and emphatic direction. For many scientific reasons, as Chip and Dan Heath show in their book *Made to Stick*, people are more likely to act on such messages. The best bosses I know have usually arrived at the same conclusion on the basis of experience. A.G. Lafley, the effective, humane, and wise CEO of Procter & Gamble, falls into that camp. One of his favorite pieces of advice is to keep it "*Sesame Street* simple."

Remember: You may have spent an hour carefully crafting an e-mail and many hours making sure that all your direct reports know what is happening and what they can do—but even so, any one of them may have just glanced at the e-mail and become so agitated when you spoke that the message simply didn't stick. I suspect that Lafley has repeated some of his *Sesame Street*-simple messages so often that they bore him silly. But he is smart enough to know that there is always someone in the room who hasn't absorbed the point before—and that those hearing it for the tenth time can only conclude he really means it. If you aren't saying the same things over and over again, and aren't a bit bored with yourself, it may be that you aren't repeating yourself enough or your messages are overly complex.

Affording Control

People don't embark on careers to feel powerless. The whole point of work is to achieve outcomes and have impact. That's why people are so deeply frustrated when events seem to render them helpless. As a boss in a bad economy, you may not be able to give people much control over *what* happens, but it's important that they have as much say as possible in *how* and *when* it happens.

During overwhelming times, a good boss finds ways to keep up a drumbeat of accomplishments, however minor. The organizational theorist Karl Weick shows in his classic article "Small Wins" that when an obstacle is framed as too big, too complex, or too difficult, people are overwhelmed and freeze in their tracks. Yet when the same challenge is broken down into less daunting components, people proceed with confidence to overcome it. One boss I know at a troubled company recently launched a crucial sales campaign that in the best case may enable the company to raise everyone's pay and in the worst case may result in huge layoffs and possibly even the company's demise. It was a bet-the-farm move that had every chance of paralyzing his already spooked people. But rather than allowing them to fret about the scale of the effort, he kicked it off by asking the team to jot down on sticky notes every discrete task required to do the campaign right. Then he sorted the notes on a whiteboard according to whether each task was "easy" or "hard" in the team's opinion. It turned out that more than half were easy and could be accomplished within a few days. He then asked for a volunteer to take responsibility for each of the easy tasks and requested that when a task had been accomplished, its owner report back to the entire group via e-mail. Not only was a lot of progress made in the following week, but the flurry of "got it done" e-mails dramatically lowered people's collective anxiety, enhanced their collective energy, and gave them confidence that the hard tasks, too, could be handled.

Showing Compassion

Jerald Greenberg, a management professor at The Ohio State University, provides compelling evidence that compassion affects the bottom line in tough times. Greenberg studied three nearly identical manufacturing plants in the Midwest that were all part of the same company; two of them (which management chose at random) instituted a temporary 10-week pay cut of 15% after the firm had lost a major contract. At one of the two, the executive who conveyed the news did so curtly, announcing, "I'll answer one or two questions, but then I have to catch a plane for another meeting." At the other one, the executive who broke the news gave a detailed and compassionate explanation, along with apologies and multiple expressions of remorse. He also spent a full hour answering questions about why the cost cutting was necessary, who would be affected, and what steps workers could take to help themselves and the plant. Greenberg found fascinating effects on employee theft rates. At the plant where the curt explanation was given, the rate rose to more than 9%. But at the plant where management's explanation was detailed and compassionate, it rose only to 6%. (At the third plant, where no pay cuts were made, the rate held steady at about 4% during the 10-week period.)

After pay was restored at the two plants, theft rates at both returned to the original level of about 4%. Greenberg's interpretation is that employees stole more at the two plants where cuts were made to "get even" with their employer, and stole the most at the plant where managers exhibited a lack of compassion because they had more to get even for. This suggests that compassion from a boss adds corporate value—in good times and in bad. What's more, it's free.

Compassion can and does take many forms. At its heart it is as simple as adopting the other person's point of view, understanding his anxiety, and making a sincere effort to soothe it. A manager who had just completed a second round of layoffs shared with me a valuable lesson she had learned about empathy: A boss delivering bad news to a subordinate is, by definition, at a later point in the emotional cycle of reacting to it. By the time they talk, the boss has already worked through the shock, anger, and embarrassment; gone through all the scenarios in her head; made decisions; and come to terms with them. "You need to remind yourself," this manager said, "that the person across the table is hearing the news for the first time and is just starting that process." Not only will that person be unready to engage with the considerations the boss is outlining, but he may be appalled at how dispassionately they are presented. And as a boss, don't assume that an employee's initial reaction will persist. This manager told me that employees who had hugged her and thanked her sometimes came back to scream at her a few days later, after the shock wore off. Others, who had reacted angrily, came back to apologize and then hugged and thanked her.

Compassion is most important when it helps people retain their dignity. When layoffs and closings are unavoidable, tending to the emotional needs of people who are let go is essential both for them and for those who survive the cuts. One of the worst things a boss can do after a layoff is to bad-mouth or in any other way demean those who have departed. Even if you believe that you've cut out the deadwood, saying so will anger and demoralize your remaining employees and may drive the best of them to jump ship. Ray Kassar, the former CEO of Atari, generated a lot of anger in the 1980s when, after a deep layoff, he told survivors that the weak people were gone and only good people were left. Many survivors we interviewed perceived the layoffs as purely political and believed that some great people had been let go.

Unfortunately, not every executive has learned from Kassar's blunder. Elon Musk, the CEO of Tesla Motors, which makes and sells electric sports cars that cost about $100,000 each, cut some 10% of his workforce in late 2008. Although he was more subtle than Kassar, Musk made pretty clear that he was getting rid of the weakest people. "One of the steps I will be taking," he wrote that October, "is raising the performance bar at Tesla to a very high level, which will result in a modest reduction in near term headcount. To be clear, this doesn't mean that the people that depart Tesla for this reason wouldn't be considered good performers at most companies—almost all would. However, I believe Tesla must adhere more closely to a special forces philosophy at this stage of its life if we aspire to become one of the great car companies of the 21st century."

Musk's statement was interpreted both inside and outside the company as misguided and destructive. But it teaches us a valuable lesson: Before making a statement, stop to consider how it will sound to an upset and touchy person.

The Sign of a Great Boss

Bosses who increase predictability, understanding, control, and compassion for their people will allow employees to accomplish the most in a time of anxiety—and will earn their deep loyalty. A manager who provides all four will be perceived as "having people's backs." That's a good phrase to keep in mind when you know your people are feeling vulnerable, because it will inform all your actions, big and small. Years ago, during a downturn, I was a consultant to a supply-chain group within Hewlett-Packard called SPaM. The company was struggling to cut costs and had eliminated free doughnuts in the morning—a long-standing tradition. At the time, people at SPaM were working very long hours and bringing in quite a bit of money. They were remarkably annoyed the day the doughnuts disappeared, and remarkably happy, proud, and motivated when their boss, Corey Billington, found some internal SPaM funds to bring the doughnuts back. I remember sitting in the coffee room one morning right after their return. One of the first employees to come in, who barely recognized me, couldn't help commenting when he saw the spread: "Isn't it great to have your boss in your corner?"

Bosses who do this sort of thing usually do it on many levels. I still hear stories about Bill Campbell's leading the senior team of Go, a troubled pen-based computing company, in the early 1990s. Campbell is affectionately known as "the coach," because he was head coach of the Columbia football team in the 1970s, and is widely respected in Silicon Valley. (He is known to be one of Steve Jobs's most trusted advisers.) He played a major role in growing many companies and mentoring dozens of bosses, from Google's executive team to the Netscape cofounder Marc Andreessen to the entrepreneur and venture capitalist Randy Komisar. I've talked extensively with Komisar about how Campbell fought to save Go during those tough times and why not a single member of its top team left, even though things kept looking worse and worse. When I asked Komisar to explain exactly how Campbell made people feel so loyal and invested in saving the company, he pounded out this impressive list:

- He would hug people when he happened upon them.

- He would always make some hackneyed joke that each of us could have stepped in and completed after a short while, but it showed genuine warmth.

- His door was open and he would have one-on-ones at all levels of the company, being careful not to undermine his managers.

- He explicitly rewarded loyalty, singling people out in company presentations and building up those who showed real commitment.

- He punished disloyalty and lack of dedication by withdrawing his attention and warmth. Everyone could feel it.

- He insisted on excellence and held people accountable. He rewarded performance not with money but with responsibility and the status that came with his attention.

- He made himself visible.

- He would stand up for his people and organization with others (investors, partners, competitors), and everyone knew the stories and retold them until they became legendary.

The venture capitalist John Doerr told *Fortune*, "Bill was at his finest when we were winding down Go. His most important thing was that we take care of the people, that they leave that venture with dignity." Many members of the team went on to successfully lead other companies such as VeriSign, Netscape, and LucasArts Entertainment. Not only did people remain loyal to Campbell throughout the struggle to save Go, but most alums, including Komisar, look back on those days as one of the finest periods of their lives.

Bill Campbell's story contains a lesson that bosses often forget, given the tunnel vision and desperation provoked by tough economic times: Win or lose, if your people believe that you are always on their side, it will come back to help you—but if they believe you are willing to sell them out at the drop of a hat, it can haunt you down the road.

Originally published in June 2009. Reprint R0906E

Layoffs That Don't Break Your Company

by Sandra J. Sucher and Shalene Gupta

TWO GREAT FORCES ARE TRANSFORMING the very nature of work: automation and ever fiercer global competition. To keep up, many organizations have had to rethink their workforce strategies, often making changes that are disruptive and painful. Typically, they turn to episodic restructuring and routine layoffs, but in the long term both damage employee engagement and company profitability. Some companies, however, have realized that they need a new approach.

Consider the case of Nokia. At the beginning of 2008 senior managers at the Finnish telecom firm were celebrating a one-year 67% increase in profits. Yet competition from low-cost Asian competitors had driven Nokia's prices down by 35% over just a few years. Meanwhile, labor costs in Nokia's Bochum plant in Germany had risen by 20%. For management, the choice was clear: Bochum had to go. Juha Äkräs, Nokia's senior vice president of human resources at the time, flew in to talk about the layoff with the plant's 2,300 employees. As he addressed them, the crowd grew more and more agitated. "It was a totally hostile situation," he recalls.

The anger spread. A week later 15,000 people protested at Bochum. German government officials launched an investigation and demanded that Nokia pay back subsidies it had received for the plant. Unions called for a boycott of Nokia products. The news was filled with pictures of crying employees and protesters crushing

Nokia phones. Ultimately, the shutdown cost Nokia €200 million—more than €80,000 per laid-off employee—not including the ripple effects of the boycott and bad press. The firm's market share in Germany plunged; company managers estimate that from 2008 to 2010 Nokia lost €700 million in sales and €100 million in profits there.

In 2011, when Nokia's mobile phone business tanked, its senior leaders decided they needed to restructure again. That would involve laying off 18,000 employees across 13 countries over the next two years. Chastened by their experience in Germany, Nokia's executives were determined to find a better solution. This time, Nokia implemented a program that sought to ensure that employees felt the process was equitable and those who were laid off had a soft landing.

One of us, Sandra, has spent eight years researching best practices for workforce change in global multinational companies. She has seen that all too frequently companies do bad layoffs, do layoffs for the wrong reason, or worse, do both. By "bad," we mean layoffs that aren't fair or perceived as fair by employees and that have lasting negative knock-on effects. The job cuts in Bochum ignited outrage because Nokia had generated so much profit the year before. Consequently, they were seen as unjust and took a steep toll on Nokia's reputation and sales. And when we say "wrong reasons," we mean done to achieve short-term cost cuts instead of long-term strategic change. In 2008, Nokia did have the right reasons, but it still suffered because of its process.

Some governments, recognizing the massive damage layoffs create, have written laws protecting employees against them. For example, a number of European countries require companies to provide a social or economic justification before they can conduct layoffs. France, however, recently eliminated the requirement to provide an economic justification, and in the United States companies can conduct layoffs at will. Regardless of how easy it might be to cut personnel, executives should remember that doing so will have consequences.

The research clearly shows that bad layoffs and layoffs for the wrong reasons rarely help senior leaders accomplish their goals. In

Idea in Brief

The Situation

Automation and fierce competition are forcing many companies to resort to frequent rounds of layoffs.

The Problem

All too often, layoffs done for short-term gain damage employee engagement and actually reduce profitability.

The Better Way

Some companies have developed workforce change strategies that make sparing use of staff reductions and ensure that when they do happen, the process feels fair and the company and the affected parties are set up for success.

this article, we'll present a better approach to workforce transitions—one that makes sparing use of staff reductions and ensures that when they do happen, the process feels fair and the company and the affected parties are set up for success.

Why Layoffs Are Ineffective

If Nokia's story sounds familiar, albeit a little more colorful than usual, that's because it is. In the United States alone, the Bureau of Labor Statistics reports, 880,000 to 1.5 million people were laid off annually from 2000 to 2008 and from 2010 to 2013 (the last year data was compiled). This happened even when the economy was expanding. During 2009, the height of the Great Recession, 2.1 million Americans were laid off. Globally, unemployment rose by 34 million from 2007 to 2010, data from the International Labour Organization shows.

Layoffs have been increasing steadily since the 1970s. In 1979 fewer than 5% of *Fortune* 100 companies announced layoffs, according to McMaster University sociology professor Art Budros, but in 1994 almost 45% did. A McKinsey survey of 2,000 U.S. companies found that from 2008 to 2011 (during the recession and its aftermath), 65% resorted to layoffs. Today layoffs have become a default response to an uncertain future marked by rapid advances in technology, tumultuous markets, and intense competition.

Yet other data on layoffs should give companies pause. In a 2012 review of 20 studies of companies that had gone through layoffs, Deepak Datta at the University of Texas at Arlington found that layoffs had a neutral to negative effect on stock prices in the days following their announcement. Datta also discovered that after layoffs a majority of companies suffered declines in profitability, and a related study showed that the drop in profits persisted for three years. And a team of researchers from Auburn University, Baylor University, and the University of Tennessee found that companies that have layoffs are twice as likely to file for bankruptcy as companies that don't have them.

All too frequently, senior managers dismiss such findings. Some argue that since companies do layoffs because they're already in bad shape, it's no surprise that their financial performance may not improve. Layoffs are so embedded in business as a short-term solution for lowering costs that managers ignore the fact that they create more problems than they solve.

Companies that shed workers lose the time invested in training them as well as their networks of relationships and knowledge about how to get work done. Even more significant are the blighting effects on survivors. Charlie Trevor of University of Wisconsin–Madison and Anthony Nyberg of University of South Carolina found that downsizing a workforce by 1% leads to a 31% increase in voluntary turnover the next year. Meanwhile, low morale weakens engagement. Layoffs can cause employees to feel they've lost control: The fate of their peers sends a message that hard work and good performance do not guarantee their jobs. A 2002 study by Magnus Sverke and Johnny Hellgren of Stockholm University and Katharina Näswall of University of Canterbury found that after a layoff, survivors experienced a 41% decline in job satisfaction, a 36% decline in organizational commitment, and a 20% decline in job performance.

While short-term productivity may rise because fewer workers have to cover the same amount of work, that increase comes with costs—and not only to the workers. Quality and safety suffer, according to research by Michael Quinlan at the University of New South Wales, who also found higher rates of employee burnout and turnover. Meanwhile, innovation declines. For instance, a study of one *Fortune* 500 tech firm done by Teresa Amabile at Harvard Business School discovered that after the firm cut its staff by 15%, the number of new inventions it produced fell 24%. In addition, layoffs can rupture ties between salespeople and customers. Researchers Paul Williams, M. Sajid Khan, and Earl Naumann have found that customers are more likely to defect after a company conducts layoffs. Then there's the effect on a company's reputation: E. Geoffrey Love and Matthew S. Kraatz of University of Illinois at Urbana–Champaign found that companies that did layoffs saw a decline in their ranking on *Fortune*'s list of most admired companies.

Employees who are downsized pay a price beyond the immediate loss of their jobs. Wayne Cascio, a professor at the University of Colorado, points to the Labor Department's survey of workers who were laid off during 1997 and 1998, an economic upswing. Most were worse off a year later: Only 41% had found work at equal or higher pay, 26% had found jobs at lower pay, and another 21% were still unemployed or had left the workforce entirely. The effects follow people throughout their lives. A 2009 Columbia University study that looked at employees who had been laid off during the 1982 recession showed that 20 years later they were still earning 20% less than peers who had kept their jobs. The aftershocks aren't limited just to earnings: According to a study by Kate Strully, an assistant professor at SUNY, laid-off employees have an 83% higher chance of developing a new health condition in the year after their termination and are six times more likely to commit a violent act.

The Search for Alternatives

A few companies have been experimenting with better ways to handle their changing workforce needs. Take AT&T. In 2013 the company's leaders concluded that 100,000 of its 240,000 employees were working in jobs that would no longer be relevant in a decade. Instead of letting these employees go and hiring new talent, AT&T decided to retrain all 100,000 workers by 2020. That way, the company wouldn't lose the knowledge the employees had developed and wouldn't undermine the trust in senior management that was necessary to engagement, innovation, and performance. So far, the results seem very positive. In a 2016 HBR article, AT&T's chief strategy officer, John Donovan (now CEO of AT&T Communications), noted that 18 months after the program's inception, the company had decreased its product development cycle time by 40% and accelerated its time to revenue by 32%. Since 2013, its revenue has increased by 27%, and in 2017 AT&T even made *Fortune*'s 100 Best Companies to Work For list for the first time.

In her work, Sandra has studied seven companies that, like AT&T, have successfully pursued alternatives to traditional layoffs. An analysis of their experiences reveals that an effective workforce change strategy has three main components: a philosophy, a method, and options for a variety of economic conditions.

A philosophy

A workforce change philosophy serves as a compass for senior leaders. It builds on a company's values and spells out the commitments and priorities the company will abide by as it implements change. A philosophy helps leaders answer the following questions:

- What value do we believe employees contribute to our business and its success?

- What expectations do we have for employees' engagement, loyalty, flexibility, and ability to adapt and grow?

- What do we owe employees as a fair exchange for what they have given us?

- How can employees help us develop and implement workforce change?

The philosophy of the French tire maker Michelin, for example, includes hiring people for their potential rather than for the job. In its labor relations policy, the company describes its commitment to employees' long-term growth. Each employee is assigned a career manager who oversees his or her development and helps make sure it aligns with Michelin's needs.

The company also has a defined approach to workforce change and restructuring. Michelin's labor relations policy described it like this in 2013:

> *Restructures are inevitable in certain circumstances in order to maintain the company's global competitiveness. These restructures must, as far as possible, take place at times when the company's health allows mobilization of adequate resources to attenuate the social consequences. Whenever possible, staff at the entities concerned and their representatives are invited to work together to seek and suggest solutions for restoring competitiveness and reducing overcapacity, which may open up an alternative to closing an activity or site. When restructuring is unavoidable, it must be announced as soon as possible and carried out according to the procedures negotiated with the staff representatives. The ensuing changes on a personal level must be supported for as long as is necessary to ensure that the reclassified employees find a satisfactory solution in terms of standard of living, stability, family life and self-esteem.*

When Nokia was contemplating that massive workforce reduction in 2011, its senior leaders articulated a philosophy with four core values:

1. *We will accept our responsibility as the driver of the local economies and aim for the highest of aspirations in supporting our previous and current employees.*
2. *We will take an activist role and lead the program with our brand, expertise, and resources in the key areas that matter most.*
3. *We will involve all of the relevant parties in ᴛɦe program design and operations.*
4. *We will communicate openly towards all stakeholders, including employees, unions, government, and local stakeholders, even when we do not know the full answers.*

As Nokia's philosophy highlights, workforce change can affect many people beyond employees. A company must communicate its intent directly without leaving any of them in the dark or piecing together scraps of information to figure out what the future holds.

A method
Having a clear methodology will allow companies to explore alternatives to layoffs, and if they cannot be avoided, minimize the harm they cause. To establish one, firms need to address three questions:

- How will we plan for workforce change on an ongoing basis?
- Who will be accountable for managing and supervising it?
- What metrics should we use to determine whether our actions are effective?

In 2013, Michelin's CEO, Jean-Dominique Senard, asked the members of his team to turn the insights they'd gathered from the previous decade's restructuring efforts into a formal process for workforce change. As a result, Michelin integrated three planning processes—product planning, territory planning, and restructuring planning—into one. The product-planning groups project their anticipated production for the next five years, and then the territories identify which regions will have too much or too little production capacity and what technologies each factory will need. The restructuring plans come out of the dialogue between the product and territory heads. For example, in October 2013, Michelin determined that it would have overcapacity for truck tire production in its Budapest factory and decided to close it in mid-2015. By making that call early, Michelin's team had time to carefully plan objectives for the shutdown and create a way to reduce the impact on the affected employees (something we'll discuss more later).

Michelin has set up an accountability structure that clearly delineates who is responsible for what. The company's executive committee, led by the CEO, oversees workforce change globally. Because more than 50% of Michelin's factories and most of its workforce reductions are in Europe, a European restructuring committee supports the executive committee. It identifies factories that should be closed or downsized and directly oversees all European restructurings. Finally, Michelin establishes a committee for each factory that will be affected, consisting of regional and country executives who are responsible for implementing the restructuring plan. Two senior executives at headquarters—a director of restructuring and a director of product planning—coordinate the entire process.

Like any other good strategy, an effective workforce change strategy includes goals against which success can be measured. An example of these comes from Honeywell. In the 2001 recession, right before Dave Cote became its CEO, the company laid off 25,000 employees, or nearly 20% of its staff. Sales fell by 11% from 2000 to 2002. When the recession hit in 2008, and it looked as if more workforce changes might be required, Cote set two goals: to improve on Honeywell's poor performance during the 2001 recession, and to be in a stronger position than its competitors when the recovery came.

To measure the first goal, Cote decided to compare the company's sales, net income, and free cash flow figures for the two recessions. As it turns out, the firm was able to improve substantially on all three measures. In 2009 Honeywell's sales were 39% higher than its 2002 sales, its free cash flow was 94% higher, and its net income was more than six times higher. To monitor progress on the second goal, performance against competitors, financial data providers developed two measures: the percent change in operating income from the 2007–2008 peak to 2011, and total stock returns in 2012. At +1.8%, Honeywell had the highest postrecession increase in operating margins (versus −4.5% to +1% among its peers). And at 75.28, Honeywell also had the highest three-year total stock return in 2012, 50% better than its closest competitor's return and four times better than the lowest-performing competitor's.

Options for a variety of economic conditions
A workforce change strategy should anticipate three different scenarios: a healthy present, short-term economic volatility, and an uncertain future.

A healthy present. In the immediate term, senior leaders should practice disciplined hiring and use stringent performance metrics to build a strong organization that can weather change. A lean approach to staffing will help companies avoid yo-yoing between overexuberant hiring during growth and damaging staff reductions when demand falls.

Before Cote began his turnaround in 2002, Honeywell had a policy of hiring freely during good times and then cutting jobs in downturns. The drastic head count reduction of 2001 was too much for Cote, who responded by introducing hiring controls. Senior leaders had to justify how staff additions would help new-product or market development, and if they couldn't, had to trim costs elsewhere to fund the hires.

Too often managers use layoffs as an excuse to avoid difficult discussions about performance. Many companies practice "rank and yank" layoffs to thin out weaker employees, often on an annual basis, but it's more productive to use meaningful performance reviews and employee development plans to cultivate a base of high performers. Lincoln Electric, an arc-welding products and consumables manufacturer headquartered in Cleveland, Ohio, has had a no-layoff policy in its U.S. operations since 1958. Part of the reason it maintains that policy is that it has a reputation for high-quality and efficient staff, thanks to very strict performance standards and a rigorous evaluation process. Employees are assessed twice a year in five areas. Performance is competitive within departments, and performance ratings are tied to a merit-based compensation system. Employees who fall in the bottom 10% receive an improvement plan and, if they remain there consistently, are eventually let go.

Short-term volatility. Experienced managers develop a range of ways to reduce costs without resorting to destructive layoffs. Three approaches implemented by Honeywell, Lincoln Electric, and Recruit Holdings, a Japanese human resources and advertising media conglomerate, demonstrate how much room there is for creative management during downturns.

During the Great Recession, Cote used furloughs instead of layoffs at Honeywell. Having weathered three recessions when he was at GE, he had developed a sense for when a business cycle might run its course. Two years before any sign that the economy was in trouble, he began to pull back on hiring. Once the recession hit, Honeywell furloughed employees for one to five weeks, providing unpaid or partially compensated leaves, depending on local labor regulations. According to an article by Tom Starner in *Human Resource Executive*, the company's finance department estimated that furloughs saved Honeywell the equivalent of 20,000 jobs.

In a 2013 article he wrote for HBR, Cote explained, "I've never heard a management team talk about how the choices they make during a downturn will affect performance during a recovery. . . . I kept reiterating that point: There will be a recovery, and we need to be prepared for it." Furloughs allowed Honeywell to retain the talent it needed when demand resurged and helped it stay profitable throughout the recession and achieve strong growth during the five years after the recovery.

In 2000, Recruit Holdings developed an innovative system, Career View, through which it hires employees with nontraditional backgrounds as three-year contractors. The system helps Recruit achieve two goals: expand its reach outside Japan's major cities and increase workforce flexibility—a real feat given that Japanese companies traditionally don't do layoffs. The program targets rural employees who lack the education and experience to land a job at a major Japanese corporation, hiring them as sales associates for regional offices near their hometowns. Six months after joining Recruit, these contractors meet with career counselors to discuss their goals. They also receive detailed performance reviews that lay out the skills they're developing, the skills they need to get their next job—generally at another company—and what they can do to bridge the gap between the two. Approximately 90% of Career View employees are able to get another job at the end of their three-year stints, and Recruit is able to expand its regional presence and adjust its sales staffing up or down according to the economic cycle.

Lincoln can avoid layoffs because it requires employees to accept flexible assignments. Employees are expected to work extra hours when demand ramps up, and they understand that they'll work shorter hours when it ramps down. In addition, they can be reassigned to any other job, including one with a lower salary, for the duration of a downturn. When orders fell during the Great Recession, for instance, Lincoln moved some factory workers into sales. Those employees developed a deeper understanding of Lincoln, and customers benefited because the factory workers had a thorough knowledge of the firm's products. In addition, during economic lulls, Lincoln's leaders automatically shift their priorities to initiatives they aren't able to fully attend to when business is booming, such as developing quality improvements, scrap-reduction programs, research and development projects, and maintenance tasks—all enabled by the availability of skilled employees who have more time to help out when demand falls.

An uncertain future. Market shifts, new technologies, and new competition can require companies to do major restructuring. Before considering a layoff, they should see if they can take a cue from AT&T's transformation.

Michelin, for one, has embraced transformations as part of its workforce strategy. When Bertrand Ballarin joined the company, in 2003, one of his first jobs was to manage a factory in Bourges, France, that was going to be shut down. He gathered its managers and union reps, explained the situation, and gave them a year to come up with a plan to save the plant. After analyzing how other Michelin plants were producing airplane tires, one of three product lines handled in the factory, the team concluded that the Bourges facility had a better, more consistent industrial process for making them than the other plants did. The team successfully argued that Bourges should specialize in airplane tires and get a new research center to aid product development.

In 2013, Michelin began applying the lessons from Bourges to a factory in Roanne, France, that was at risk of being shut down. From October 2014 to March 2015, more than 70 individuals, including leaders from headquarters, union representatives, plant managers, and employees, met to develop a transformation strategy for Roanne. Rather than closing the facility and laying off its employees, Michelin agreed to put €80 million into creating a new line of premium tires there; the head count would fall from 850 to 720 employees through natural attrition. Instead of the traditional four teams working Monday to midday Saturday, the plant would reorganize into five teams that kept operations running seven days a week around the clock, and all employees would work six additional days a year. These changes allowed the plant to flex production up or down by 12% according to market conditions. In addition, Michelin dedicated €2 million to programs for improving the quality of management and work-life balance—issues that had emerged during the transformation strategy planning—for the plants' employees.

However, there are times when a transformation isn't possible or the transformation itself results in layoffs. In these cases, companies have to ensure that employees are treated fairly. This isn't just about being a Good Samaritan. Datta found that companies tended to get better financial results after a layoff when employees thought it was handled equitably and done for strategic reasons rather than cost cutting.

Let's look again at what happened at Nokia in 2011, when its senior leaders realized the company needed another restructuring. Then-chairman Jorma Ollila was determined to avoid another Bochum. To help the company do so, a small team of senior leaders developed Nokia's Bridge program, which aimed to see that as many employees as possible had a new opportunity lined up the day their current job ended. Nokia opened Bridge centers in the 13 countries where the layoffs would take place. The program outlined five paths employees could choose from:

1. **Find another job at Nokia.** In order to avoid favoritism, selection committees were formed to determine which employees to retain, instead of having local managers choose.

2. **Find another job outside Nokia.** The centers offered outplacement services, including career coaching, résumé workshops, career fairs, and networking events.

3. **Start a new business.** Individual employees or teams could present business proposals to win grants of up to €25,000. Employees were given two months to develop their plans, as well as support such as coaching and mentoring, networking introductions, and training. Nokia took no stake in any of the funded businesses.

4. **Learn something new.** Nokia offered training grants for business-management and trade-school courses in many areas, including restaurant management, cosmetology, construction, and firefighting.

5. **Build a new path.** The company offered financial support to employees who had personal goals they wanted to accomplish, such as volunteering.

Nokia spent €50 million on Bridge, or about €2,800 per employee. That accounted for just 4% of the €1.35 billion it spent on restructuring from 2011 to 2013. As a result of the program, 60% of the 18,000 affected workers knew their next step the day their jobs ended. Overall, 85% of the Finnish Bridge participants said they were satisfied with the program, while 67% of global employees said they were. Furthermore, the layoff candidates and the remaining employees maintained or improved quality levels throughout the restructuring. Employees at the sites that were targeted for downsizing achieved €3.4 billion in new-product revenues, one-third of new-product sales—the same proportion they had brought in before. Employee engagement scores in all areas of the company held steady throughout the restructuring. And, unlike the situation in Bochum, there were no labor actions of any kind in the 13 countries where the layoffs happened. By all accounts Nokia had indeed found a better approach to workforce change.

In 2017, three years after selling its devices and services business to Microsoft, Nokia used an enhanced version of the Bridge program to handle its latest restructuring. Microsoft Finland has rolled out a similar program. And Finland's government has even taken cues from Bridge and incorporated ideas from it into legislation outlining what companies that conduct layoffs are required to provide for affected employees.

One of the biggest questions organizations face as they grapple with a constantly shifting economic landscape is whether their current workforce can help them make the transitions necessary to their success. While companies tend to prioritize short-term financial results over the long-term well-being of their employees, employees are the lifeblood that enables a company to keep delivering the products and services that ultimately generate shareholder benefits. Michelin's and Nokia's experiences show that employees can and should be trusted to perform well, even when they know they might lose their jobs. For all companies, planning thoughtful workforce change instead of automatically resorting to layoffs is a better way to address the vicissitudes of technological transformation and intensifying competition.

Originally published in May–June 2018. Reprint R1803K

Getting Reorgs Right

by Stephen Heidari-Robinson and Suzanne Heywood

CHANCES ARE YOU'VE EXPERIENCED at least one and possibly several company reorganizations. Reorgs can be a great way to unlock value: Two-thirds of them deliver at least some performance improvement, and with change in the business environment accelerating, they are becoming more and more common. As John Ferraro, the former COO of Ernst & Young, told us, "Every company today is being disrupted and so must frequently reorganize to keep up with the incredible pace of change. Those that can do this well will thrive in the current environment and be tomorrow's winners."

At the same time, few reorgs are entirely successful. According to a McKinsey survey we conducted, more than 80% fail to deliver the hoped-for value in the time planned, and 10% cause real damage to the company. More important, they can be damned miserable experiences for employees. Research suggests that reorgs—and the uncertainty they provoke about the future—can cause greater stress and anxiety than layoffs, leading in about 60% of cases to noticeably reduced productivity. In our experience, this occurs because the leaders of reorgs don't specify their objectives clearly enough, miss some of the key actions (for example, forgetting processes and people in their focus on reporting lines), or do things in the wrong order (such as choosing the way forward before assessing the strengths and weaknesses of what they already have). Yet the pitfalls they succumb to are common and entirely predictable. (See the sidebar "Why Reorgs Fail.")

During our careers we have seen many reorgs, read lots of books and articles about which type of organization companies should adopt, and watched countless fads come and go. But we've found precious little advice on how to actually run a reorg. Many practitioners assert that reorgs are so fluid and dynamic that it would be naive and counterproductive to try to impose a process on them. Our conclusion, based on experience and analysis, is the opposite: *How* you go about your reorg is as important as—and sometimes more important than—*what* you do.

To help maximize the value and minimize the misery of reorgs, we have developed a simple five-step process for running them. We don't claim that this is rocket science; indeed, we're proud to assert that it is not. But we do know that companies need to take a more systematic approach if reorgs are to deliver on their potential. And we have personally advised companies through the five steps in more than 25 reorganizations—companies with 100,000 employees or a handful, in the Americas, Europe, the Middle East, Asia, and Africa. In fact, survey data shows that companies using this process are three times as likely as others to achieve their desired results.

Step 1: Develop a Profit and Loss Statement

A reorganization is not some esoteric pursuit but a business initiative like any other—similar to a marketing push, a product launch, or a capital project. So you should start by defining the benefits, the costs, and the time to deliver. Remember that the costs are not just those of employees and consultants involved in the reorg; they also include the human cost of change and the disruption it can create in your business. We have accumulated data on these factors for 1,800 reorgs. Previous reorgs in your company, and the experience of employees who have worked elsewhere, can help you estimate the impact.

It may seem like common sense to weigh costs and benefits, but according to McKinsey research, only 15% of executives set detailed business targets for their reorgs, and 17% of reorgs are launched at the whim of an executive or because the leadership team believes the company needs to be shaken up—reasons that typically lead to problems. Both the objective of the reorg and the process for running it should be as fair, transparent, and reasonable as possible. Not

Idea in Brief

The Problem

Most reorganizations fail to deliver on their initial promise, for several reasons: They run into employee resistance, they're not given sufficient resources, and they distract people from day-to-day work.

What's Missing

The biggest reason for disappointing results, though, is that few organizations follow a rigorous, disciplined process—even though

reorgs are a common occurrence in large companies.

The Solution

The authors propose a five-step process: Begin with a profit and loss estimate, inventory your strengths and weaknesses, consider multiple options for the new organization, focus special attention on execution, and assume you'll need to make course corrections.

---

only is that right for your employees, but it will make them much more likely to accept, get behind, and improve your ideas. (See the sidebar "Communicating the Reorg.")

Let's consider the case of an international media company. Its reorg started with an exercise to define the revenue-improvement opportunity worldwide. At the time, it was a federation of local businesses with no net growth. Teams of company strategists and business experts estimated that a more integrated global approach could significantly grow flat revenue and set a specific target for the reorg. The cost of internal project support and external consultants was agreed on, and a timeline was proposed: The new organization would ideally be set up and running within a year—in time to deliver results in the latter half of a new three-year business plan. A reorg P&L had been constructed.

Step 2: Understand Current Weaknesses and Strengths

No surgeon would start operating on a patient before conducting tests and reaching a diagnosis. And when excising a tumor, he or she would be careful to avoid removing healthy tissue. So should it be with a reorg. Unfortunately, this step is often skipped, which means that changes at best have no impact and at worst undermine previous strengths. Those companies that do take the time to self-diagnose before embarking on major surgery typically rely on interviews with senior executives to get input. That's a good place to start, but we would recommend adding an electronic survey, which will enable you to capture a companywide range of input and to see the differences between headquarters and the front line and between levels and geographies. In addition, since reorgs are all about performance improvement, take time to understand how outcomes vary across the business. For example, if you have multiple sales teams, which one is most successful and why? These inputs will help you decide what to retain, what to roll out elsewhere, and what to change.

The media company interviewed 23 leaders across all parts of the business, using a "card sort" in which 40 attributes of the existing organization—such as innovation, local responsiveness, and leadership bench strength—were written on cards, and interviewees were asked to categorize them as "significant issue," "somewhat of an issue," or "not an issue." This process highlighted problems that the company was having finding the right people to fill roles, sharing information across geographies, and incentivizing innovation. Yet the company scored well on P&L accountability and local responsiveness—strengths that needed to be preserved. (Although these interviews were helpful, we realized in retrospect that the responses represented too thin a slice of the organization. In subsequent reorgs elsewhere in the company, we used electronic survey tools that captured a much wider range of opinions across levels, business units, and geographies.)

Step 3: Consider Multiple Options

The next step is to decide on the design of your new organization. You can take one of two approaches. You can change the entire organizational model—for example, organizing by customer segments instead of along geographical lines. That approach is best if your organization is completely broken (although such cases are rare) or is facing a fundamental market shift that cannot be navigated under the current model. Or you can change only those elements that don't work—for example, altering the executive board process for financial approvals, removing a layer of middle management, or upgrading your frontline leaders while leaving the rest of the organization unchanged. That approach is best when the overall organization works well or the focus is on cutting costs. The analysis you conducted in the first two steps will help you make the choice. If in doubt, choose the second approach.

A common mistake in this step is to focus on *what the organization looks like* (its reporting structure, for instance) and forget about *how it works* (management and business processes and systems; and the numbers, capabilities, mindsets, and behaviors of its people). In our experience, the latter is usually more important than the former.

Finally, you should explicitly choose from a number of options for exactly how to restructure your organization. Any solution has its downsides; only by weighing alternatives will you see what you might gain and what you might lose. Too often leaders realize late in the day that they missed something in the original design. If they insist on adding it later, the company may end up with a push-me-pull-you design that blunts the effectiveness of the new organization and unnecessarily complicates people's lives.

At the media company, the top 12 global business leaders gathered offsite to debate the relative merits of three options. They were assigned to teams—one for each option—and asked to advocate for their given option (no negatives allowed) and to answer questions from the other teams. Leaders who were expected to dislike a particular model were deliberately put on the team for that model: For example, the most autonomous local leaders were put on the team for the most centralized option.

During the debate it became increasingly clear that the most centralized model was the only one that would provide sufficient benefits to justify the disruption and the human cost of the change. At the end of the meeting, nine of the 12 leaders voted for that option, and the specific concerns of the remaining three were accounted for in the detailed design. After the exercise, the CEO reflected, "There is always more than one right answer, so how you bring people along and get them behind the new organization is really important.

Communicating the Reorg

TO BE CONSIDERATE of your employees and get their buy-in, the process needs to be fair and transparent.

Plan communications across all steps of the reorg
Start with transparent information: what will happen, when, and whom it will affect. Try to excite people only after it's clear what they will be doing (in step 4). If you try earlier, they won't listen, and you'll come across as detached.

Focus your communications on topics that matter to your people, not just to you
Sadly, few of your employees will care as much as you do about ROIC. You have to find something about the change that motivates them. Elon Musk says of the companies he's founded and their organization going forward, "People at Tesla, SolarCity, and SpaceX feel that they are doing things that matter: If we can advance sustainable energy by 10 years, that is 10 years of less carbon."

Make sure communication is in person, not just in e-mail cascades
Too often your carefully crafted e-mails will get no further than your direct reports' in-boxes. Make sure your leaders are spelling out the practicalities of the reorg for their staffs and answering employees' questions.

Communication should be two-way
This is especially true in steps 4 and 5, when you are trying to get the details of the reorg right and ensure that it is working properly. On-the-ground feedback from your staff is essential. Reflecting on his experience of reorganizations, John Browne, the former CEO of BP, told us, "Your people are sometimes aware of what is going on before you are, so you need to listen to them."

Through the workshop, we came to a good answer, and—perhaps more important—we brought our leadership team along with us."

Step 4: Get the Plumbing and Wiring Right

After step 3, most executives stand back, trusting their teams to handle the details of the new organization and the transition plan. External consultants usually clock off at this point as well. Yet we've repeatedly found—and a 2014 McKinsey survey confirmed—

that step 4 is the hardest part of the reorg to get right. The secret is knowing all the elements that need to change and planning the changes in the right sequence. For example, you must create new job descriptions before the jobs can be filled, and they must be filled before you start location moves, potentially across countries. Similarly, you need to agree on how your P&L will be managed before you can allocate costs and revenues, and only then can you design the required IT changes, test them, and ultimately implement them. All this takes effort, and if you miss something in any area of the detailed design—structural changes, processes and systems, or people—you may either hold up the whole reorg or find that your new organization has been launched half born. In many cases the organization has changed but the systems (notably the P&L) have not, and leaders are left driving a fast car with no steering wheel.

Executives at the media company put in extra effort at this stage. The CEO continued to spend significant time on the reorganization; leaders were appointed to their new roles before the switchover so that they could begin to own and steer the work; and the reorg project team members moved from managing the process out of HQ to visiting the regional businesses that would be most difficult to transition and working with the local management teams to hammer out the plan. In particular, they took pains to understand how the P&L of each local business broke down and who would be responsible for each revenue or cost lever in the new organization. Of course, this process highlighted previously unappreciated challenges—such as the fact that customer segmentation, which was clear at the global level, was sometimes less clear in a few countries where customer groups blended together; and the need to account for acquisitions that were midway through integration when the detailed design was developed. This prompted the company to make some tweaks and exceptions to its new structure and processes and to lengthen transition periods for some units. But its leaders stood fast on something we've found to be a fundamental rule for successful reorgs: 80% of the business (by revenue, profit, and people) must make the change, and the exceptions must not be allowed to hold up progress for the rest.

Why Reorgs Fail

A MCKINSEY SURVEY OF 1,800 EXECUTIVES identified the most common pitfalls for reorganizations (in order of frequency).

1. Employees actively resist the changes.

2. Insufficient resources—people, time, money—are devoted to the effort.

3. Employees are distracted from their day-to-day activities, and individual productivity declines.

4. Leaders actively resist the changes.

5. The org chart changes, but the way people work stays the same.

6. Employees leave because of the reorg.

7. Unplanned activities, such as an unforeseen need to change IT systems or to communicate the changes in multiple languages, disrupt implementation.

Step 5: Launch, Learn, and Course Correct

No matter how much thought and preparation you put into a reorg, it's unrealistic to expect that it will work perfectly from the beginning. As Nancy McKinstry, the CEO of another client—the information services company Wolters Kluwer—says, "You have to live with and digest it, and rapidly course correct when you find issues." That doesn't mean you need to do a 180 in the design as soon as you hit a snag. But you do need to encourage everyone to spot and point out the new organization's teething problems, openly debate solutions, and implement the appropriate fixes as soon as possible, in line with the logic of your original plans.

The media company's reorg was altered in several ways after the launch. One activity around developing content, which had been allocated to a new business line, was returned to its original unit, because synergies that had been persuasive on paper turned out to be less impressive in practice. Back-office activities, untouched by the revenue-focused reorg, were further consolidated afterward, bringing cost savings into the mix.

Within three years of the reorg, the company had met its goal: The issue of flat revenue had been addressed and the growth target met.

If you're contemplating a reorg, you owe it to your shareholders and employees to follow a rigorous process rather than winging it, as so many leaders do. You'll make better decisions, keep your people more involved and engaged, and capture more value.

Originally published in November 2016. Reprint R1611F

Reigniting Growth

by Chris Zook and James Allen

MOST SUCCESSFUL COMPANIES EVENTUALLY FACE a predictable crisis that we call *stall-out*—a sudden large drop in revenue and profit growth or a collapse of once high shareholder returns to well below the cost of capital. Stall-out occurs when the growth engine that powered a company to success stops working. This rarely happens because the business model has suddenly become obsolete—a common misconception. Rather, our research shows that the business has almost always become too complex, most often owing to bureaucracy that slows the company's metabolism, or internal dysfunction that distorts information and hampers managers' ability to make rapid decisions and take swift action on them. When we talk to executives about the symptoms of stall-out, their words vary, but the reasons remain the same. *We've lost touch with customers. We're drowning in process and PowerPoint. We have no shortage of opportunities, but somehow we can no longer act decisively. What was once such a high-energy ride now feels like trying to pilot a plane with no thrust and unresponsive controls.*

In an analysis of 8,000 global companies, we found that two-thirds of those successful enough to reach $500 million in revenue faced stall-out over the 15 years ending in 2013—including notables such as Panasonic, Time Warner, Carrefour, Bristol-Myers Squibb, Alcatel-Lucent, Philips, Sony, and Mazda. More alarming still, for 50 large companies in prolonged stall-out, we found that the onset had usually been sudden: Momentum fell sharply over just a year or two, with growth rates dropping from double digits to low single digits or even negative numbers—a finding consistent with past research (see "When Growth Stalls," HBR, March 2008).

To be sure, external forces put pressure on incumbent companies. Strategy—the external chessboard of business—still matters. Yet competitive strategies are more similar than they used to be, more easily copied, and of shorter duration. The roots of success or failure increasingly lie in the ability of companies to remain fast, perceptive, innovative, and adaptable. Internally thriving companies can respond to shifts in their competitive environments, identifying—and executing—strategies that sustain their dominance. When we polled 377 business leaders, 94% of those in companies with revenue of more than $5 billion told us that internal dysfunction—not lack of opportunity or unmatchable competitor capabilities—was now the main barrier to their continued profitable growth.

Yes, stall-out may be predictable, but it can be overcome. We argue in a forthcoming book that most companies with sustainable growth share attitudes and behaviors: (1) They view themselves as business insurgents, fighting in behalf of underserved customers; (2) they have an obsession with the front line, where the business meets the customer; and (3) they foster a mindset that includes a deep sense of responsibility for how resources are used and for long-term results. Because these qualities are most vibrant in companies led by bold, ambitious founders, we call them "the founder's mentality." Since 2000, returns to shareholders in large public companies where the founder is still involved have been three times those for other companies. But any leadership team can harness the revitalizing effects of the founder's mentality. In some cases, a once dominant mindset has been lost over time and may need to be rebuilt from a few vestiges. But these three qualities can help any company restart its growth engine by removing gunk and complexity that has built up over the years, inhibiting the clean execution of strategy.

1. Rediscover Your Insurgent Mission

When stall-out occurs, it is almost always connected to creeping complexity. "No single bad decision or tactic or person was to blame," Howard Schultz said after returning to the CEO position at Starbucks in 2008 amid shrinking revenue, collapsing margins, and

Idea in Brief

The Problem

Growing companies often face the predictable crisis of stall-out—a sudden large drop in revenue and profit growth. The culprits are usually complexity and bureaucracy.

The Solution

Leaders need to rediscover the "founder's mentality"—attitudes and behaviors that are strongly associated with founding management teams and can revitalize the business.

The Principles

Stalling companies should drastically reduce complexity and excess cost, refresh the mission, and configure the organization to focus obsessively on the business's front line. Finally, they should instill an owner's mindset that eschews bureaucracy and celebrates speed and accountability.

---

a decline in stock price of more than 75%. Starbucks's stall-out was sudden and dramatic, he acknowledged, but it resulted from damage that had been "slow and quiet, incremental, like a single loose thread that unravels a sweater inch by inch."

To begin tackling stall-out, companies need to strip away complexity and excess cost in order to liberate resources, narrow focus, and harness the vigor that drove the company's early growth. We studied 10 successful rescue-and-rebirth operations and found that all of them involved reducing operating costs by at least 8% and sometimes more than 25%.

Successful attacks on complexity are led from the top down and proceed in a sequence. First the company must shed noncore assets and businesses. Next it must develop a simpler strategy for the remaining businesses. Then it can attack complexity in the core processes. Finally, it can focus on reducing product complexity in design, variations, and customization. We've seen leadership teams attempt transformation in the reverse order, only to become trapped in details and wear down the organization before getting to what really makes most transformations successful: reducing high-level complexity and cost.

We have found that as companies grow in size, internal budget processes become democratic, spreading resources evenly across businesses and opportunities. But democratic investment in the face of crisis is a sure path to mediocrity. The opposite is needed to reverse stall-out. At companies where it was avoided, leaders had made bold investment decisions to redifferentiate the company, usually establishing a major new capability that set off waves of growth.

Once back in shape, companies must renew their view of themselves as business insurgents. This does not require promoting a martial culture or abusing the metaphor of "waging war" on competitors. Rather, companies should view their customers as underserved and their industries as setting insufficient standards, and should constantly emphasize what is special about themselves. Bold goals—not just the aim of living to fight another day—will sustain growth. As they become very large, organizations may find maintaining an insurgent mission hard, but it's not impossible. Google's mission to "organize the world's information," for example, is at once specific to Google and nearly infinite in its ambition.

A company should even be prepared to shrink significantly if that's what is needed to regroup, redeploy, and restart profitable growth. Consider the case of Perpetual, the oldest trust company in Australia, which recovered from stall-out by reducing its operating costs by 20%, stripping away noncore businesses, and rejuvenating around its founder's original mission.

Established in 1886 to manage trusts and estates for Australia's scions, Perpetual led the market for most of its history. But as it grew, it diversified into 11 new business areas, and by 2011 the company was struggling. Its share price had fallen from a high of $84 to $24 in only four years. Profits were down by nearly 70%, with no bottom in sight. Shareholders were calling publicly for a major overhaul, and the company had hired its third CEO in 12 months, Geoff Lloyd.

When he arrived, he "found an organization that was internally competitive and externally cooperative," Lloyd told us. "We had grown incredibly complex over time by entering more businesses, and we were not the leader in most of them." Lloyd concluded that to save Perpetual, he would have to return the company to its core mission: the protection of Australia's wealth. That, he realized, meant making the company "faster, more confident, and, above all, simpler."

Lloyd began by replacing 10 of the 11 members of the management team with people who had no vested interest in past decisions. With his new staff in place, he launched Transformation 2015, five initiatives designed to bring about swift complexity reduction at all levels. One was the "portfolio" initiative, which reduced the number of businesses from 11 to three (just two businesses were responsible for about 95% of profits), cut real estate holdings by half, and eliminated more than 100 legacy funding structures. Another, the "operating model" initiative, reduced the staff at headquarters by more than 50%. Lloyd and his team found that back-office support, staff functions, and redundant controls accounted for 60% of total costs. In other words, the company was putting only 40% of its money toward sales, customer service, and investment—its core activities. Furthermore, it was relying on more than 3,000 computer systems and applications.

Cutting back—on businesses, staff, computer systems, and more—was central to the transformation plan. But Lloyd and his team also crafted a plan to gain market share by investing in the company's core. He convened town hall meetings, which had never before been held at Perpetual, to discuss the company's situation and its future and to reignite enthusiasm for its core values. "We labored over the wording of our mission and strategy," Lloyd told us, explaining that he felt it was essential for employees to refocus on the founding principles of the company. In the process, he learned a remarkable thing: Perpetual's original trust business was so strong that it still had its first customer—125 years later.

His strategies brought about a stunning turnaround. Perpetual's stock price has more than doubled since Lloyd took over; employee engagement has measurably increased; the company is gaining share in its core markets; and net profits have tripled.

2. Obsess Over Your Business's Front Line

Companies that sustain growth live and breathe the front line of their business. This obsession, which can often be traced back to a strong founder, shows up in three ways: an elevated status for frontline employees, a preoccupation with individual customers at all levels of the company, and an institutional curiosity about the details of the business. A frontline obsession is most obvious in "high-touch" consumer businesses such as luxury hospitality. But the trait can exist in subtler ways in a range of industries: Consider the product obsession of Steve Jobs and the legendary attention to detail of the wine pioneer Robert Mondavi, who believed in the saying "The best fertilizer for a vineyard is the owner's footsteps."

The Home Depot, the largest home-improvement retailer in the world, provides an example of how losing a frontline obsession can lead to stall-out—and how renewing it can reignite growth. The company's initial success could be traced to its remarkable founders, Bernard Marcus and Arthur Blank, who devoted themselves to building a close advisory relationship with customers. Their corporate mantra was "Whatever it takes." The founders even trained store employees in customer service themselves. Employees, in turn, offered clinics on home improvement projects for customers and were always available in stores to provide knowledgeable advice. The strategy set the company apart and generated powerful customer loyalty, and for years The Home Depot was a major success story. From its founding, in 1978, until 2000, it consistently eclipsed its 20% annual earnings growth targets. But in December 2000, after missing an earnings target and having become increasingly concerned about antiquated systems—especially IT—in a company that was approaching $50 billion in revenue, the board of directors hired Robert Nardelli, a senior executive from GE, to introduce some big-company discipline as CEO.

Nardelli created a command-and-control environment. By early 2006, 98% of the company's top 170 executives were new to their jobs, and 56% of the new managers at headquarters had come from the outside. Fresh leadership, especially in the area of systems, was probably needed, but this changing of the guard failed to build on the deep strengths that had once made the company special and beloved by its customers. Nardelli and his team neglected customer relationships and frontline enthusiasm in favor of boosting quarterly profits. Many long-serving full-time employees were replaced by lower-paid part-time workers, and customer service collapsed. "Do it yourself," some people joked, was now "Find it yourself." When the University of Michigan released its 2006 American Customer Satisfaction Index, The Home Depot had slipped to last among major U.S. retailers. The board held meetings in the field and found a consistent pattern: concern for the future, disempowerment of longtime store employees, and a feeling that the social contract between the company, its employees, and its customers was being breached.

Greg Brenneman, the longest-serving board member and a global turnaround expert, told us, "You could see the serious trouble bubbling up under the surface. Store managers were feeling shackled by dozens of financial templates and metrics that took time away from customers and running the stores. The most experienced store employees, the real experts on plumbing or electricity, had been let go and replaced with less experienced and cheaper part-time store workers. Foot traffic, the lifeblood of any retailer, was dropping. New stores were not generating good returns, leading to further staff cuts. We were stalling out and needed to change course."

The deterioration of the customer experience was at the root of the company's woes, and thus it illuminated a path back to sustainable growth. In 2007 the board replaced Nardelli with Frank Blake. On his very first day on the job, Blake spoke to all employees using The Home Depot's internal television station and quoted extensively from Marcus and Blank's book, *Built from Scratch*. In particular, he highlighted two of their charts. One listed their core values, and the other gave pride of place, at the top of an inverted triangle, to the company's front line: its stores, where customers and employees interact.

Many of Blake's first initiatives focused on restoring the "orange-apron cult": knowledgeable store employees, easily identifiable by their aprons, who focused on high levels of customer service. Taking advice from Marcus, Blake also began anonymously visiting stores on "undercover missions," as he called them. These proved so valuable that he instructed his senior executives to adopt a "management by walking about" approach, something most had never done before.

Like Lloyd at Perpetual, Blake then set out to reduce complexity, restructuring the businesses and closing money-losing stores—essentially, shrinking to grow. He also increased the employee bonus pool by a factor of seven, rehired some veterans, and asked store managers to return to the pre-Nardelli policy of giving out honor badges to employees who had been exceptionally attentive to customers.

Eight years ago The Home Depot had stalled out and was facing the prospect of free fall. But as of the end of 2015, thanks to Blake's renewal of the founders' mentality, the company has reenergized its employees and repersonalized its customer experience—a return to core principles that has driven the company's stock from about $25 a share in 2009 to more than $130 by December 2015.

3. Instill an Owner's Mindset

The third factor in reversing stall-out involves a management idea that first came into vogue 40 years ago: the owner's mindset. Designed to instill balance-sheet discipline and accountability by aligning employees and shareholders, this concept is frequently misunderstood. Too often, it implies an incumbent's mindset: a concern with hunkering down and extracting value from the existing business, and a loss of interest in innovating, serving customers uniquely, and fully valuing frontline employees.

At its best, the owner's mindset focuses on the long term, has a strong bias toward speed and action, and embraces personal responsibility for employees' actions and for how resources are used. The power of the owner's mindset is central to the rise of the private equity industry—a reaction against the bureaucracy, poor cost management, and complexity that beset many large companies. When we analyzed the returns of deals within several private equity funds, we found that businesses sold by large public companies in which management had seemingly lost the incentives of ownership subsequently earned nearly 50% more than the others. After private equity firms had restored the owner's mindset, these companies benefited from increased speed, reduced bureaucracy, a more

How to Get Started

Here are some ways to prepare your team to reignite growth.

Create a "founder's mentality" scorecard

Manage it as a strategic asset. Does your mission keep you fighting in behalf of your customers? Does your company focus on the front line of the business? Do employees embrace an owner's mindset that eschews bureaucracy, is focused on speed, and demands personal accountability?

Benchmark against your most successful upstart competitors

Are they winning on speed and cost? Commit as a leadership team to closing the gap.

Launch a campaign against bureaucracy

Look for management layers and processes that have outlived their usefulness. Eliminate them.

Get the leadership team out of the office

The front line is where the answer to a growth stall-out is most likely to reside.

Reexamine the precepts and practices of your founders or early leaders

When was the company at its best? What has been lost along the way that needs to be restored?

Look outside for help inside

You might reach out to retired founders or acquire fast-growing, founder-led young companies.

---

critical evaluation of noncore businesses, and an improved management of costs.

A case in point is Dell, the best-performing large company of the 1990s. It began to stall out a decade later, when some of the advantages of its legendary direct sales model began to narrow, and the company saw its market value decline from $107 billion in 1999 to just under $25 billion in 2013—a 77% drop. When Michael Dell returned as CEO to renew the company he'd founded, he concluded that he could more effectively make the changes he wanted if he took the company private, which he did in partnership with Silver Lake in 2013.

"In going private," he told us, "it's amazing how we have been able to speed things up. We simplified meeting structures, went to a board of directors with just three members, and increased our appetite for risk. When big committees talk about risk, they talk about risk committees, how risk is bad, the mitigation procedures of risk, and the reaction of the analysts. For us risk is now about innovation and success. It has been very energizing to our 100,000 employees to feel the long-term focus coming back into the company."

Customer satisfaction scores have rebounded, and Dell's employee satisfaction scores are the highest in the company's history. Its core businesses are outgrowing their industry peers again, and Dell is investing heavily to redefine its model for the long term.

Going private is not for all, of course. An owner's mindset can be instilled without taking the business off the market. Companies can generate "mini-founder" experiences by, for example, creating franchises with direct ownership stakes or encouraging employees to create internal startups that might later be spun off. They can encourage investors with a more long-term focus and link executive pay more closely to long-term performance measures. They can change the timing of internal meetings to increase the speed of decision making. (Some leadership teams, for instance, hold Monday meetings and Tuesday follow-ups with the aim of removing blockages to important decisions and actions.) They can reach outside the company to partner with insurgents and perhaps eventually acquire them. Or they can bring founders into the company through acquisition and work to retain them and their entrepreneurial energy. This has been the approach of companies such as Cisco, Google, and eBay.

Initially a huge success story, and one of the first dot-coms to radically scale up, eBay stalled out in the late 2000s—a victim of Amazon and other online retail competitors and of its own diversification, which included acquiring Skype. Its aging e-commerce auction model seemed vulnerable to competitors, and its share price had fallen from $59 in 2004 to a low of $10 in 2009.

When John Donahoe became the CEO at eBay, he recognized that to get the company moving again, he would have to divest noncore businesses, revamp eBay's e-commerce platform, and, most important, shift its focus to a hotbed of innovation: mobile commerce. To successfully enter the mobile space, however, he would have to turbocharge the company's innovation pipeline and capabilities—and the only way he could manage that, he told us, would be "to fill eBay with young entrepreneurs." In doing so, he was guided by a general truth about transforming stalled-out companies: Often, outside forces need to be brought in.

Not long after he took over, Donahoe began to acquire small, founder-led companies at a rate of about one every three months. He wasn't interested solely in acquisitions and technological innovations. He wanted to retain the founders and their teams, frequently so that he could move them into core-business positions. "Many of these founders like our approach," Donahoe told us, "because they can innovate at scale in eBay, and they get to expose their innovations to 130 million customers globally."

One of them was Jack Abraham, the 25-year-old founder of Milo, a shopping engine that searched stores for the best-priced merchandise. At one of the regular Friday meetings that Donahoe held with company leaders under 30, Abraham raised his hand and proposed a major innovation for the home page. Donahoe told him to go figure out what resources he needed to explore the idea. Immediately after the meeting, Abraham found five of the best developers in the company, went out for drinks with them that night, and persuaded them to leave with him the next morning for two weeks in Australia, where they would be as isolated from California headquarters as possible and could work on developing a prototype.

What they came up with blew Donahoe away. "Had we asked a normal product team," he said, "I would have gotten back hundreds of PowerPoint slides and a two-year time frame and a budget of $40 million. Yet these guys went away, worked 24/7, and built a prototype. These guys build. They do no PowerPoint. They just build."

Obviously, Donahoe's approach is best suited to fast-moving markets where incumbents need to constantly add technologies and build new capabilities. Not all these initiatives have been lasting successes. The fivefold increase in eBay's stock price during Donahoe's tenure was driven by many things, including the success and spin-off of PayPal (whose independent status has enhanced its founder's mentality), yet it is a clear example of the power of pulling in business owners from the outside and harnessing their energy and entrepreneurialism.

Stall-outs are frightening for companies—if ignored or mishandled, they can lead to lasting reversals of fortune. But like any other daunting challenge, they can also be viewed as an opportunity. When we analyzed value swings on the stock market, we found that some of the biggest upturns occur when a company is forced to return to its core and redefine it in the process. Managers need not panic when stall-out occurs. Companies that reignite their mission, renew their obsession with the front line, and instill an owner's mentality throughout the organization can reach new heights.

Originally published in March 2016. Reprint R1603F

Reinvent Your Business Before It's Too Late

by Paul Nunes and Tim Breene

SOONER OR LATER, all businesses, even the most successful, run out of room to grow. Faced with this unpleasant reality, they are compelled to reinvent themselves periodically. The ability to pull off this difficult feat—to jump from the maturity stage of one business to the growth stage of the next—is what separates high performers from those whose time at the top is all too brief.

The potential consequences are dire for any organization that fails to reinvent itself in time. As Matthew S. Olson and Derek van Bever demonstrate in their book *Stall Points*, once a company runs up against a major stall in its growth, it has less than a 10% chance of ever fully recovering. Those odds are certainly daunting, and they do much to explain why two-thirds of stalled companies are later acquired, taken private, or forced into bankruptcy.

There's no shortage of explanations for this stalling—from failure to stick with the core (or sticking with it for too long) to problems with execution, misreading of consumer tastes, or an unhealthy focus on scale for scale's sake. What those theories have in common is the notion that stalling results from a failure to fix what is clearly broken in a company.

Having spent the better part of a decade researching the nature of high performance in business, we realized that those explanations missed something crucial. Companies fail to reinvent themselves not necessarily because they are bad at fixing what's broken, but because they wait much too long before repairing the deteriorating bulwarks of the company. That is, they invest most of their energy managing to the contours of their existing operations—the financial S curve in which sales of a successful new offering build slowly, then ascend rapidly, and finally taper off—and not nearly enough energy creating the foundations of successful new businesses. Because of that, they are left scrambling when their core markets begin to stagnate.

In our research, we've found that the companies that successfully reinvent themselves have one trait in common. They tend to broaden their focus beyond the financial S curve and manage to three much shorter but vitally important hidden S curves—tracking the basis of competition in their industry, renewing their capabilities, and nurturing a ready supply of talent. In essence, they turn conventional wisdom on its head and learn to focus on fixing what doesn't yet appear to be broken.

Thrown a Curve

Making a commitment to reinvention before the need is glaringly obvious doesn't come naturally. Things often look rosiest just before a company heads into decline: Revenues from the current business model are surging, profits are robust, and the company stock commands a hefty premium. But that's exactly when managers need to take action.

To position themselves to jump to the next business S curve, they need to focus on the following.

The hidden competition curve

Long before a successful business hits its revenue peak, the basis of competition on which it was founded expires. Competition in the cell phone industry, for instance, has changed several times—for both manufacturers and service providers—from price to network coverage to the value of services to design, branding, and applications.

Idea in Brief

High-performance companies rethink their strategies and reinvent their operating models before debilitating stalls set in.

In order to successfully jump from one financial S curve to the next, they do three things differently from their less-successful peers:

Focus On the Edges
They pay attention to the edge of the company and the edge of the market, to avoid the myopia that long-running success engenders.

Shake Up the Top Team
They change the makeup of the senior team earlier, and more radically, than their competitors do.

Maintain Surplus Talent
When other companies are cutting staff to cut costs, they go in the opposite direction: They cultivate serious talent with the capacity to grow new businesses.

Jumping the S curve

High performers are well on their way to new-business success by the time their existing businesses start to stall.

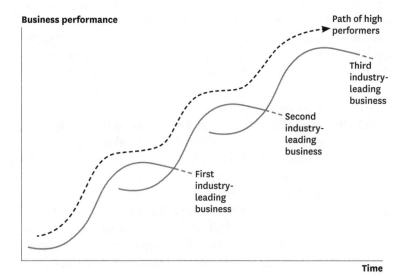

Business performance

Path of high performers

Third industry-leading business

Second industry-leading business

First industry-leading business

Time

The first hidden S curve tracks how competition in an industry is shifting. High performers see changes in customer needs and create the next basis of competition in their industry, even as they exploit existing businesses that have not yet peaked.

Netflix, for example, radically altered the basis of competition in DVD rentals by introducing a business model that used delivery by mail. At the same time, it almost immediately set out to reinvent itself by capturing the technology that would replace physical copies of films—digital streaming over the internet. Today Netflix is the largest provider of DVDs by mail and a major player in online streaming. In contrast, Blockbuster rode its successful superstore model all the way to the top, tweaking it along the way (no more late fees) but failing to respond quickly enough to changes in the basis of competition.

The hidden capabilities curve

In building the offerings that enable them to climb the financial S curve, high performers invariably create distinctive capabilities. Prominent examples include Dell with its direct model of PC sales, Wal-Mart with its unique supply chain capabilities, and Toyota with not just its production method but also its engineering capabilities, which made possible Lexus's luxury cars and the Prius. But distinctiveness in capabilities—like the basis of competition—is fleeting, so executives must invest in developing new ones in order to jump to the next capabilities S curve. All too often, though, the end of the capabilities curve does not become apparent to executives until time to develop a new one has run out.

Take the music industry. The major players concentrated on refining current operations; it was a PC maker that developed the capabilities needed to deliver digital music to millions of consumers at an acceptable price. High performers are continually looking for ways to reinvent themselves and their market. P&G long ago recognized the untapped customer market for disposable diapers. The company spent five years perfecting the capabilities that would allow diapers to be priced similarly to what customers were then paying services to launder and deliver cloth diapers. Amazon.com CEO Jeff Bezos notes that it takes five to seven years before the seeds his company plants—things

Why Now?

WHY DO ECONOMIC SLOWDOWNS call for innovation and reinvention? Reduced sales and increased discounting tend to squash companies' revenue S curves. Worse, the S curves do not stretch back out as conditions improve. Companies lose ground in four key areas:

Intellectual Property

Patent offices don't put years back on the clock just because a company's sales tapered off in a bad economy. This can have a devastating effect on, for instance, pharmaceuticals, where generics constantly challenge proprietary drugs as patents expire.

Technology

Economic downturns can slow the introduction of new technologies, but not for long. Witness the fate of some manufacturers of plasma televisions, which have been forced to exit the business under the double whammy of the downturn and steady improvements in LCD and LED sets.

Competition

Companies looking to grow sales in a recession must take market share from competitors. As they press advantage, already weakened companies face possible extinction. In the movie-viewing market, for instance, companies that dominate newer channels have driven bricks-and-mortar retailers into bankruptcy.

Consumer Tastes

Novelty wears off, regardless of the economy. Even though they've bought less during the downturn, consumers accustomed to the idea of "fast fashion," for example, will not be interested in last year's styles.

---

like expanding beyond media products, working with third-party sellers, and going international—grow enough to have a meaningful impact on the economics of the business; this process requires foresight, early commitment, and tenacious faith in the power of R&D.

The hidden talent curve

Companies often lose focus on developing and retaining enough of what we call serious talent—people with both the capabilities and the will to drive new business growth. This is especially true when the business is successfully humming along but has not yet peaked. In such circumstances, companies feel that operations can be leaner (they've moved far down the learning curve by then) and meaner, because they're under pressures to boost margins. They reduce both head count and investments in talent, which has the perverse effect of driving away the very people they could rely on to help them reinvent the business.

The high performers in our study maintain a steady commitment to talent creation. The oil-field services provider Schlumberger is always searching for and developing serious talent, assigning "ambassadors" to dozens of top engineering schools around the world. These ambassadors include high-level executives who manage large budgets and can approve equipment donations and research funding at those universities. Close ties with the schools help Schlumberger get preference when it is recruiting. Not only does Schlumberger keep its talent pipeline flowing, but it's a leader in employee development. In fact, it is a net producer of talent for its industry, a hallmark of high performers.

By managing to these hidden curves—as well as keeping focused on the revenue growth S curve, it must be emphasized—the high performers in our study had typically started the reinvention process well before their current businesses had begun to slow. So what are the management practices that prepare high performers for reinvention? Let's look first at the response to the hidden competition curve.

Edge-Centric Strategy

Traditional strategic-planning methods are useful in stretching the revenue S curve of an existing business, but they can't help companies detect how the basis for competition in a market will change.

To make reinvention possible, companies must supplement their traditional approaches with a parallel strategy process that brings the edges of the market and the edges of the organization to the

The hidden S curves of high performance

Three aspects of a business mature—and start to decline—much faster than financial performance does. They need to be reinvented before you can grow a new business.

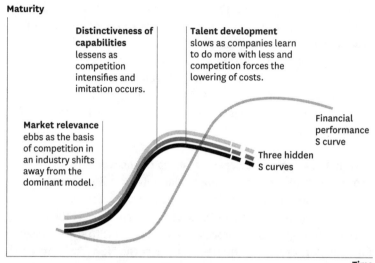

Maturity

Distinctiveness of capabilities lessens as competition intensifies and imitation occurs.

Talent development slows as companies learn to do more with less and competition forces the lowering of costs.

Market relevance ebbs as the basis of competition in an industry shifts away from the dominant model.

Financial performance S curve

Three hidden S curves

Time

center. In this "edge-centric" approach, strategy making becomes a permanent activity without permanent structures or processes.

Moving the edge of the market to the center

An edge-centric strategy allows companies to continually scan the periphery of the market for untapped customer needs or unsolved problems. Consider how Novo Nordisk gets to the edge of the market to detect changes in the basis of competition as they're occurring. For example, through one critical initiative the pharma giant came to understand that its future businesses would have to address much more than physical health. The initiative—Diabetes Attitudes, Wishes, and Needs (DAWN)—brings together thousands of primary care physicians, nurses, medical specialists, patients, and delegates from major associations like the World Health Organization to put the individual—rather than the disease—at the center of diabetes care.

Research conducted through DAWN has opened Novo's eyes to the psychological and sociological needs of patients. For example, the company learned that more than 40% of people with diabetes also have psychological issues, and about 15% suffer from depression. Because of such insights, the company has begun to reinvent itself early; it focuses less on drug development and manufacturing and more on disease prevention and treatment, betting that the future of the company lies in concentrating on the person as well as the disease.

Moving the edge of the organization to the center

Frontline employees, far-flung research teams, line managers—all these individuals have a vital role to play in detecting important shifts in the market. High performers find ways to bring these voices into the strategy-making process. Best Buy listens to store managers far from corporate headquarters, such as the New York City manager who created a magnet store for Portuguese visitors coming off cruise ships. Reckitt Benckiser got one of its most successful product ideas, Air Wick Freshmatic, from a brand manager in Korea. The idea was initially met with considerable internal skepticism because it would require the company to incorporate electronics for the first time—but CEO Bart Becht is more impressed by passion than by consensus.

If strategy making is to remain on the edge, it cannot be formalized. We found that although low and average performers tend to make strategy according to the calendar, high performers use many methods and keep the timing dynamic to avoid predictability and to prevent the system from being gamed.

As quickly as competition shifts, the distinctiveness of capabilities may evaporate even faster. By the time a business really takes off, imitators have usually had time to plan and begin their attack, and others, attracted to marketplace success, are sure to follow.

How, then, do companies build the capabilities necessary to jump to a new financial S curve?

Change at the Top

Some executives excel at running a business—ramping up manufacturing, expanding into different geographies, or extending a product line. Others are entrepreneurial—their strength is in creating new markets. Neither is inherently better; what matters is that the capabilities of the top team match the firm's organizational needs on the capabilities S curve. Companies run into trouble when their top teams stay in place to manage the financial S curve rather than evolve to build the next set of distinctive capabilities.

Avoiding that trap runs counter to human nature, of course. What member of a top team wants to leave when business is good? High performers recognize that a key to building the capabilities necessary to jump to a new financial S curve is the early injection of new leadership blood and a continual shake-up of the top team.

Early top-team renewal

Consider how the top team at Intel has evolved. Throughout its history, the semiconductor manufacturer has seen its CEO mantle rest on five executives: Robert Noyce, Gordon Moore, Andy Grove, Craig Barrett, and current CEO Paul Otellini. Not once has the company had to look outside to find this talent, and the transitions have typically been orderly and well orchestrated. "We discuss executive changes 10 years out to identify gaps," explains David Yoffie, who has served on the Intel board since 1989.

Simple continuity is not Intel's goal in making changes at the top, however; evolving the business is. For instance, when Grove stepped down from the top spot, in 1998, he was still a highly effective leader. If continuity had been Intel's overwhelming concern, Grove might have stayed for another three years, until he reached the mandatory retirement age of 65. But instead, he handed the baton to Barrett, who then implemented a strategy for growing Intel's business through product extensions.

About the Research

AT ACCENTURE, WE HAVE BEEN conducting the High Performance Business research program since 2003. Starting from the premise that all performance is relative, we examined sets of peer companies. Previous research on high performance had compared companies head-to-head across industries, but that approach ignored the differences in average profitability, maturity, and risk from one industry to another, making it a contest among industries rather than among companies.

We settled on 31 peer sets for our initial study, encompassing more than 800 companies and representing more than 80% of the market capitalization of the Russell 3000 Index at the time. We analyzed performance in terms of 13 financial metrics to assess growth, profitability, consistency, longevity, and positioning for the future. In most cases, we applied the metrics over a 10-year span.

The businesses that performed extraordinarily well over the long term had all made regular transitions from maturing markets to new, vibrant ones. To find out how these organizations were able to maintain a high level of performance, we conducted years of follow-on investigation, creating special teams from our industry and business-function practice areas. Team members' expertise and experience was supplemented by contributions from independent researchers and scholars.

Today, the program includes regional and global studies of high performance, to take into account the explosive success of many emerging-market companies.

Indeed, each of Intel's CEOs has left his mark in a different way. Grove made the bold decision to move Intel away from memory chips in order to focus on microprocessors, a transition that established the company as a global high-tech leader. Since he took the helm, in 2005, Otellini has focused on the Atom mobile chip, which is being developed for use in just about any device that might need to connect to the web, including cell phones, navigation systems, and even sewing machines (for downloading patterns).

Through structured succession planning, Intel ensures that it chooses the CEO who is right for the challenges the company is facing, not simply the person next in line. And by changing CEOs early, the company gives its new leadership time to produce the reinvention needed, well before deteriorating revenues and dwindling options become a crisis.

Balance short-term and long-term thinking

Ensuring that the team is balanced with a focus on both the present and the future is another critical step in developing a new capabilities curve. When Adobe bought Macromedia in 2005, then-CEO Bruce Chizen took a hard look at his senior managers to determine which of them had what it took to grow the company to annual revenues of $10 billion. What he found was a number of executives who lacked either the skills or the motivation to do what was necessary. Consequently, Chizen tapped more executives from Macromedia than from Adobe for key roles in the new organization. Those choices were based on Adobe's future needs, not on which executives were the most capable at the time.

Chizen wasn't tough-minded just with others. At the relatively young age of 52, and only seven years into his successful tenure, he handed over the reins to Shantanu Narayen, his longtime deputy. The timing might have seemed odd, but it made good sense for Adobe: The company faced a new set of challenges—and the need for new capabilities—as it anticipated going head-to-head against larger competitors like Microsoft.

In other cases, the executive team might need to gather fresh viewpoints from within the organization to balance long-established management thinking. Before Ratan Tata took over at India's Tata Group, in 1991, executives had comfortably ruled their fiefdoms for ages and rarely retired. But the new chairman began easing out those complacent executives (not surprisingly, some of their departures were acrimonious) and instituted a compulsory retirement age to help prevent the future stagnation of his senior leadership. The dramatic change opened dozens of opportunities for rising in-house talent who have helped Tata become India's largest private corporate group.

Organize to avoid overload

Finally, high performers organize their top teams so that responsibilities are more effectively divided and conquered. Three critical tasks of senior leadership are information sharing, consulting on important decisions, and making those decisions. Although many companies have one group that performs all three functions, this can easily become unwieldy.

An alternative approach, which we observed in many high performers, is to split those tasks—in effect, creating teams nested within teams. At the very top are the primary decision makers—a group of perhaps three to seven people. This group then receives advice from other teams, so hundreds of people may be providing important input.

Surplus Talent

Business reinvention requires not just nimble top teams but also large numbers of people ready to take on the considerable challenge of getting new businesses off the ground and making them thrive. High performers take an approach that is, in its way, as difficult as changing out top leadership before the company's main business has crested: They create much more talent than they need to run the current business effectively—particularly talent of the kind that can start and grow a business, not just manage one. This can be a hard sell in the best of times, which is probably why so many avoid it.

One of the signs that a company has surplus talent is that employees have time to think on the job. Many of our high performers make time to explore a regular component of their employees' workweek. (Think Google and 3M.) Another is a deep bench—one that allows promising managers to take on developmental assignments and not just get plugged in where there is an urgent need. High performance companies aggressively search out the right type of candidate and then take action to strengthen individuals for the challenges ahead.

Hire for cultural fit

High performance companies begin with the expectation that they are hiring people for the long term—a perspective that fundamentally alters the nature of their hiring and development practices. They don't just look for the best people for the current openings; they recognize that cultural fit is what helps ensure that someone will perform exceptionally well over time.

One company that gets this right is the Four Seasons Hotels and Resorts. It specifically looks for people who will thrive in a business that treats customers like kings—because, quite literally, some guests could be. "I can teach anyone to be a waiter," says Isadore Sharp, CEO of the luxury hotel chain in his book *Four Seasons: The Story of a Business Philosophy.* "But you can't change an ingrained poor attitude. We look for people who say, 'I'd be proud to be a doorman.'"

Reckitt Benckiser also puts cultural fit at the top of its hiring priorities. Before candidates begin the application process, they can complete an online simulation that determines whether they are likely to be a good match with the firm's exceptionally driven culture. The candidates are presented with business scenarios and asked how they would respond. After reviewing their "fit" score, they can decide for themselves whether they want to continue pursuing employment with the company.

Prepare for challenges ahead

Making sure that new employees are fit to successfully navigate the tough stretches in a long career requires something we call stressing for strength. At low-performer companies, employees may find themselves wilting when faced with unexpected or harsh terrain. High performers create environments—often challenging ones—in which employees acquire the skills and experience they will need to start the company's next S curve. The goal is partly to create what our Accenture colleague Bob Thomas, in his book on the topic, calls "crucible" experiences. These are life-changing events, whether on the job or not, whose lessons help transform someone into a leader.

Crucible experiences can—and should—be created intentionally. When Jeff Immelt was still in his early 30s and relatively new in his career at GE, he was tapped by then-CEO Jack Welch and HR chief Bill Conaty to deal with the problem of millions of faulty refrigerator compressors—despite his lack of familiarity with appliances or recalls. Immelt later said he would never have become CEO without that trial-by-fire experience.

Give employees room to grow

After choosing and testing the right employees, companies must give them a chance to develop. To truly enable them to excel in their work, companies should take a hard look at exactly what people are required to do day by day.

UPS has long known that its truck drivers are crucial to its success. Experienced drivers know the fastest routes, taking into account the time of day, the weather, and various other factors. But the turnover rate for drivers was high, partly because of the hard physical labor required to load packages onto the trucks. So UPS separated out that task and gave it to part-time workers, who were more affordable and easier to find, allowing a valuable group of employees to concentrate on their capabilities and excel at their jobs.

Companies can also use organizational structure to provide employees with ample opportunities to grow. Illinois Tool Works, a global manufacturer of industrial products and equipment, is organized into more than 800 business units. Whenever one of those units becomes too large (the maximum size is around $50 million in sales), ITW splits that business, thus opening up managerial positions for young talent. In fact, it's not uncommon for ITW managers to start running a business while they're still in their 20s.

And high performance businesses aren't afraid to leapfrog talented employees over those with longer tenure. After A.G. Lafley took over at P&G, for example, he needed someone to run the North American baby-care division, which was struggling. Instead of choosing one of the 78 general managers with seniority, he reached lower in the organization and tapped Deborah Henretta. Lafley's move paid off. Henretta reversed 20 years' worth of losses in the division and was later promoted to group president of Asia, overseeing a $4 billion–plus operation.

Breaking the mold in one way or another—as leaders have done at UPS, ITW, and P&G—is critical to building surplus talent in the organization. It not only keeps key individuals (or groups, in the case of UPS's drivers) on board; it also signals to the organization as a whole that no compromises on talent will be made in order to achieve short-sighted cost savings.

Even top organizations are vulnerable to slowdowns. In fact, an economic downturn can exacerbate problems for companies already nearing the end of their financial S curve. (See the sidebar "Why Now?") Even in the best of times, business crises—whether they are caused by hungry new competitors, transformational technology, or simply the aging of an industry or a company—come with regularity. Companies in other industries may be feeling great, while your business (or industry) faces its own great depression.

In the face of all these challenges, companies that manage themselves according to the three hidden S curves—the basis of competition, the distinctiveness of their capabilities, and a ready supply of talent—will be in a much better position to reinvent themselves, jumping to the next S curve with relative ease. Those that do not are likely to respond to a stall in growth by creating an urgent and drastic reinvention program—with little likelihood of success.

Originally published in January–February 2011. Reprint R1101D

How to Protect Your Job in a Recession

by Janet Banks and Diane Coutu

IN A TROUBLED ECONOMY, job eliminations and hiring freezes seem almost routine, but when your own company's woes start to make headlines, it all hits home. Intellectually, you understand that downsizing isn't personal; it's just a law of commerce, but your heart sinks at the prospect of losing your position. While you know that passivity is a mistake, it's hard to be proactive when your boss's door is always closed, new projects are put on hold, and your direct reports look to you for reassurance. Don't panic. Even though layoff decisions may be beyond your control, there's plenty you can do.

That's what we've observed in numerous layoffs over the years and in research on how people respond to stressful work conditions. (Author Janet Banks oversaw a dozen downsizings as a vice president in human resources at Chase Manhattan Bank and a managing director at FleetBoston Financial. Author Diane Coutu studied resilience during her time as an affiliate scholar at the Boston Psychoanalytic Society and Institute.) We've seen that while luck plays an important role, survival is most often the result of staring reality in the face and making concrete plans to shape the future. Machiavellian as it may seem, holding on to your job when the economy softens is a matter of cool strategic planning. In our experience, however, even the savviest executives are ill-prepared to deal with job threats. Here's what you can do to keep your career moving and minimize the chances that you'll become a casualty.

Act Like a Survivor

A popular partner in the Brussels office of McKinsey & Company mentored hosts of junior consultants. When asked for advice on getting ahead, he always gave the same reply: "If you want to be a partner, start acting like one." The corollary of this advice is even more important: During a recession, you have to start acting like a survivor if you hope to escape the ax.

Studying the thinking of survivors reveals a surprising paradox. Though creating a plan to weather layoffs requires an almost pessimistic realism, the best thing you can do in a recession is lighten up. Keep your eye firmly on the eight ball, but act confident and cheerful. Research shows that being fun to be around really matters. Work by Tiziana Casciaro and Miguel Sousa Lobo, published in a June 2005 HBR article, "Competent Jerks, Lovable Fools, and the Formation of Social Networks," shows that while everyone prefers working with a personable superstar to an incompetent jerk, when people need help getting a job done, they'll choose a congenial colleague over one who is more capable but less lovable. We're not suggesting that you morph into Jerry Seinfeld; being congenial and fun isn't about bringing down the house. Just don't be the guy who's always in a bad mood, reminding colleagues how vulnerable everyone is. Who wants to be in the trenches with him?

Of course, putting on a good face can be psychologically exhausting when rumors of downsizing spread. Change always stirs up fears of the unknown. Will you land another job? How will you pay the mortgage? Can you find affordable health insurance? Those are all valid concerns, but if you stay positive, you'll have more influence on how things play out.

Survivors are also forward looking. Studies of concentration camp victims show that people made it through by imagining a future for themselves. The power of focusing on the times ahead is evident even among people suffering the blows of everyday life. As Freud wrote in "Mourning and Melancholia," a critical difference between ordinary grief and acute depression is that mourners can successfully anticipate a life where there will once again be joy and meaning.

Idea in Brief

Your company has a strategy for surviving hard times. But do you? In a troubled economy, layoffs can hit with frightening regularity. Sure, these decisions may be beyond your control. Yet you *can* take steps to protect your job, say Banks and Coutu.

Three practices can help you minimize the chances of becoming a casualty: 1) Act like a survivor by demonstrating confidence and staying focused on the future. 2) Give your boss hope by empathizing with him or her and inspiring your team to pull together. 3) Become a corporate citizen by taking part in meetings, outings, and new projects designed to support a reorganization.

In your job, there's no better way to look forward than to stay focused on customers, for without them no one will have a job in the future. Anticipating the needs of your customers, both external and internal, should be your top priority. Prove your value to the firm by showing your relevance to the work at hand, which may have shifted since the economy softened. Your job is less likely to be eliminated if customers find that your contribution is indispensable.

Being ambidextrous will increase your chances of survival as well. In one company we know of, senior staff members were often expected to play more than one role to keep expenses in check. When the organization's new chief operating officer decided he needed a chief of staff, he chose a person who continued to manage a human resources team, thereby eliminating the need for additional head count. Reorganizations and consolidations involve great change, so they demand versatile executives. If you're not already wearing multiple hats, start imagining how you can support your company by leveraging experience your boss may know nothing about. A marketing manager who taught school before moving into industry might volunteer to take on sales and service training responsibilities, for example. A recession can offer you plenty of opportunities to display your capabilities. Layoffs typically occur at all levels of an organization and can create vacuums above and below you.

Idea in Practice

Banks and Coutu recommend three strategies for recession-proofing your job.

Act Like a Survivor

If you want to *be* a layoff survivor, it helps to act like one:

- **Demonstrate confidence and cheerfulness.** When people need help getting jobs done, they'll choose a congenial colleague over an unlikeable one. No one wants to be in the trenches with someone who's always gloomy.

- **Keep your eye on the future.** There's no better way to look forward than to sharpen your focus on customers. Without them, no one will have a job in the future. Make anticipating customers' needs your top priority. And show how your work is relevant to meeting those needs.

- **Wear multiple hats.** To keep expenses in check, look for opportunities to play more than one role and leverage your diverse experiences. For instance, a marketing manager who had previously taught school volunteered to take on sales training responsibilities.

Give Your Boss Hope

The better your relationship with your manager, the less likely it is that you'll be cut. Strengthen that bond through these practices:

- **Empathize.** Most leaders find layoffs agonizing. By empathizing with your manager, you deepen your bond. You also

---

Finally, survivors are willing to swallow a little pride. Take the case of Anne, a manager at a large New England insurance company. (We've changed her name, as well as those of the other individuals cited in this article.) During a reorganization, Anne found herself vying for a position with a colleague who had far less industry experience than she did. When she learned that she and her department would be folded under this colleague's department, Anne realized that she had one choice if she wanted to keep her job—use her significant influence to support her new manager. So she publicly threw herself behind the colleague. In turn, he gave her the respect and the loyalty she felt she deserved. Anne's attitude demonstrated commitment to the company—something that was noticed by the management. A year later Anne got new responsibilities that led to a prestigious board appointment.

demonstrate a maturity that's invaluable—because it models good behavior for others.

- **Unite and inspire your colleagues.** This ability can prove crucial during the worst of times.

Example:
At an international financial services company that had endured a 20% staff reduction, morale had plummeted. Isaac, a learning and development VP, assembled a team of volunteers who created a live radio show that engaged even cynical employees. It included a soap opera that kept staff laughing and waiting for the next episode. And it gave executives a platform to share key information, such as the company's performance and structural changes. Morale improved, and Isaac eventually became head of management and leadership development.

Become a Corporate Citizen
Eighty percent of success is showing up. To become a corporate citizen:

- Attend all voluntary and informal meetings and corporate outings.
- Get out of your office and walk the floor to see how people are doing.
- Get on board with new initiatives; for example, by volunteering to lead a newly formed team crucial to your company's recovery strategy.

Give Your Leaders Hope

It's important to recognize that times of uncertainty are also tough for leaders. They don't enjoy having to lay off their people; most find that task agonizing. It can be stressful and time-consuming for them to sort through the various change mandates they've been given and then decide what to do. Obviously, this isn't the time to push for a promotion or to argue for a new job title. Instead, try to help the leader defend your department. If the boss is working on a restructuring plan and asks for ideas, offer some realistic solutions. Don't fight change; energize your colleagues around it.

It may sound like what Karl Marx called *false consciousness*— thinking that disempowers you because it is not in your best interest—to empathize with your boss when he or she is considering cutting your job. However, there's science to support the idea that showing empathy for people more powerful than you can be worthwhile. For example, recent mother-infant research shows that the more an infant smiles and interacts with the environment, the more active the caretaker becomes in the infant's development and survival. Although the mother-infant research has not, to our knowledge, been replicated in the workplace, psychologists have shown that so-called attachment behavior—emotional bonding—can be learned, just as emotional intelligence skills can be honed. That's good news. The better your relationship with your manager, the less likely you are to be cut, all things being equal. Your ability to empathize can demonstrate a maturity that is invaluable to the company, not least because it models good behavior for others.

The ability to unite and inspire colleagues goes a long way in the best of times; in the worst it's crucial. This was true at an international financial services company that had endured a staff reduction of 20%. In the face of low morale, the head of human resources asked Isaac, a learning and development VP, to help revive people's spirits, improve communications, and stir up some fun. Isaac quickly pulled together a small team of volunteers and created a live radio show that engaged even the most cynical members of the organization. It included a soap opera that kept staff at all levels laughing and waiting for the next episode. The show gave executives a unique platform to share information such as quarterly financial results and changes in the organization's structure. It did so much to improve morale that as a result Isaac landed the job he wanted—head of management and leadership development for the company.

Become a Corporate Citizen

Remember Woody Allen's remark that 80% of success is showing up? That is especially useful advice in a downturn. Start going to all those voluntary and informal meetings you used to skip. Be visible. Get out of your office and walk the floor to see how folks are doing. Take part in company outings; if the firm is gathering for the annual golf tournament and you can't tell a wood from an iron, then go

Preparing for the Worst: You May Still Need a Plan B

FOLLOWING THE BEST ADVICE is no guarantee that you won't get laid off. That's why you need a plan for handling a job loss.

The first key to moving on successfully is self-awareness. You'll have better luck finding a new job if you know what you're good at and what you'd really like to do, so it's wise to invest mental energy now in figuring those things out. If you have results from a Myers-Briggs test or a 360-degree assessment, revisit them to understand your strengths and weaknesses. Read self-help books to inspire your thinking, or perhaps even hire an executive coach. (Just make sure to get references and agree on fees before you start with any coach.)

Don't wait till you get laid off to update your résumé. Revise it now, so that you'll have it ready when you start approaching headhunters, former bosses and colleagues, and industry contacts for job referrals and advice. It's a good idea to begin networking with those folks now, in fact, but don't stop there. Reach out to the neighbor who's the CFO of a successful company, and dig out the old business cards from your drawer and add those names to the list of those you'll call.

Finally, think creatively about your future. Perhaps you want to go back to school, start your own business, join a smaller firm, or become a minister. That may require some downsizing of your own, but as Ellen, a consultant, told us: "Now that the kids are grown, my husband looks at the house and says it's too big for the two of us. I'm willing to scale back. Both of us want to do different things." Who knows, maybe plan B will actually be more attractive than plan A.

---

along just for fun. In tough times, leaders look for employees who are enthusiastic participants. It's not the score that counts.

Corporate citizens are quick to get on board. Consider Linda, a VP in operations, who worked in a large company that needed to cut costs. Management came up with the idea of shared service centers to avoid duplication of effort in staff functions in areas such as compensation, management training, and strategic planning. The decision was universally unpopular. Service center jobs had none of the cachet of working in small business units, where customized solutions could be developed. Headquarters staff objected to losing the elite status they'd enjoyed as corporate experts. When service center jobs were posted, many high-profile people refused to put their names forward, misjudging their own importance and hoping management would relent. But Linda saw the opportunity and applied for a service center job. The new position gave her immense visibility and was an immediate promotion. Meanwhile, many of the resisters found themselves standing without a chair when the music stopped. In contrast, Linda kept her career on track; six years later she reported directly to the president of the company.

Of course, changing your behavior or personality to survive may rub against your need for authenticity, and you may decide that it's time to move on. In that case, you can be both true to yourself and the ultimate corporate citizen by volunteering to leave the organization. Despite what the policy may be, companies will cut deals. Deals are even welcomed. It's much less painful for managers if they can help someone out the door who wants to leave rather than give bad news to someone who depends on the job. If you're a couple of years away from retirement eligibility and want to go, ask the company if it would be willing to bridge the time. Float a few balloons, but don't get greedy. Keep in mind that even if you choose to go, you may need to get another job and you'll want good references and referrals. If you've exited gracefully, odds are, your boss and others will do whatever they can to help you land on your feet.

Many forces are beyond your control in a recession, but if you direct your energy toward developing a strategy, you'll have a better chance of riding out the storm. You have to be extremely competent to make it through, but your attitude, your willingness to help the boss get the job done, and your contribution as a corporate citizen have a big impact on whether you are asked to stick around. The economy will bounce back; your job is to make sure that you do, too.

Originally published in September 2008. Reprint R0809J

Learning from the Future

by J. Peter Scoblic

HOW CAN WE FORMULATE strategy in the face of uncertainty?

That's the fundamental question leaders must ask as they prepare for the future. And in the midst of a global pandemic, answering it has never felt more urgent.

Even before the Covid-19 crisis, rapid technological change, growing economic interdependence, and mounting political instability had conspired to make the future increasingly murky. Uncertainty was so all-encompassing that to fully capture the dimensions of the problem, researchers had devised elaborate acronyms such as VUCA (volatility, uncertainty, complexity, and ambiguity) and TUNA (turbulent, uncertain, novel, and ambiguous).

In response, many leaders sought refuge in the more predictable short term—a mechanism for coping with uncertainty that research has shown leaves billions of dollars of earnings on the table and millions of people needlessly unemployed. By the start of 2020, the sense of uncertainty was so pervasive that many executives were doubling down on efficiency at the expense of innovation, favoring the present at the expense of the future.

And then the pandemic hit.

Now the tyranny of the present is supreme. A lot of organizations have had no choice but to focus on surviving immediate threats. (There are no futurists in foxholes.) But many business and political discussions still demand farsightedness. The stakes are high, and decisions that leaders make now may have ramifications for years—or even decades. As they try to manage their way through the crisis, they need a way to link current moves to future outcomes.

So how best to proceed?

Strategic foresight—the history, theory, and practice of which I have spent years researching—offers a way forward. Its aim is not to predict the future but rather to make it possible to imagine multiple futures in creative ways that heighten our ability to sense, shape, and adapt to what happens in the years ahead. Strategic foresight doesn't help us figure out *what* to think about the future. It helps us figure out *how* to think about it.

To be sure, a growing body of research has demonstrated that it is possible to make more-accurate predictions, even in chaotic fields like geopolitics. We should use those techniques to the extent we can. But when predictive tools reach their limits, we need to turn to strategic foresight, which takes the irreducible uncertainty of the future as a starting point. In that distinctive context, it helps leaders make better decisions.

The most recognizable tool of strategic foresight is scenario planning. It involves several stages: identifying forces that will shape future market and operating conditions; exploring how those drivers may interact; imagining a variety of plausible futures; revising mental models of the present on the basis of those futures; and then using those new models to devise strategies that prepare organizations for whatever the future actually brings.

Today the use of scenarios is widespread. But all too often, organizations conduct just a single exercise and then set whatever they learn from it on the shelf. If companies want to make effective strategy in the face of uncertainty, they need to set up a process of constant exploration—one that allows top managers to build permanent but flexible bridges between their actions in the present and their thinking about the future. What's necessary, in short, is not just imagination but the *institutionalization* of imagination. That is the essence of strategic foresight.

Idea in Brief

The challenge

Good strategy creates competitive advantage over time, but the uncertainty of the future makes it difficult to identify effective courses of action, particularly in the midst of a crisis. As a leader, how can you prepare for an unpredictable future while managing the urgent demands of the present?

The promise

The practice of strategic foresight provides the capacity to sense, shape, and adapt to change as it

happens. One important element of the practice is scenario planning, which helps leaders navigate uncertainty by teaching them how to anticipate possible futures while still operating in the present.

The way forward

To make effective strategy in the face of uncertainty, leaders need to institutionalize strategic foresight, harnessing the power of imagination to build a dynamic link between planning and operations.

The Limits of Experience

Uncertainty stems from our inability to compare the present to anything we've previously experienced. When situations lack analogies to the past, we have trouble envisioning how they will play out in the future.

The economist Frank Knight famously argued that uncertainty is best understood in contrast with risk. In situations of risk, Knight wrote, we can calculate the probability of particular outcomes, because we have seen many similar situations before. (A life insurance company, for example, has data on enough 45-year-old, nonsmoking white men to estimate how long one of them is going to live.) But in situations of uncertainty—and Knight put most business decisions in this category—we can only guess what might happen, because we lack the experience to gauge the most likely outcome. In fact, we might not even be able to imagine the range of potential outcomes.

The key in those situations, Knight felt, was judgment. Managers with good judgment can successfully chart a course through uncertainty despite a lack of reference points. Unfortunately, Knight had no idea where good judgment came from. He called it an "unfathomable mystery."

Of course, in something of a catch-22, conventional wisdom holds that to a large extent good judgment is based on experience. And in many uncertain situations managers do, in fact, turn to historical analogy to anticipate the future. This is why business schools use the case teaching method: It's a way of exposing students to a range of analogies—and thus ostensibly helping them develop judgment—much more quickly than is possible in the normal course of life.

But Knight's point was that uncertainty is marked by novelty, which, by definition, lacks antecedents. At the very moment when the present least resembles the past, it makes little sense to look back in time for clues about the future. In times of uncertainty, we run up against the limits of experience, so we must look elsewhere for judgment.

That's where strategic foresight comes in.

"Strange Aids to Thought"

In the United States, strategic foresight can be traced back to the RAND Corporation, a think tank that the U.S. Air Force set up after World War II. Rather than plumbing the mystery of judgment, RAND scholars hoped to replace it with the "rational" tools of quantitative analysis. But as they grappled with the military demands of the postwar world, they could not escape the fact that nuclear weapons had fundamentally changed the nature of warfare. Two countries, the United States and the Soviet Union, had acquired the ability to destroy each other as functioning civilizations. And because no one had ever fought a nuclear war before, no one knew how best to fight (or avoid) one.

One RAND analyst, who approached the problem of a potential apocalypse with a glee that made him a model for Stanley Kubrick's Dr. Strangelove, was a mathematician named Herman Kahn. In the atomic age, Kahn realized, military strategists faced uncertainty to an absolutely unprecedented degree. "Nuclear war is still (and hopefully will remain) so far from our experience," he wrote, "that it is difficult to reason from, or illustrate arguments by, analogies from history."

How, then, Kahn asked, could military strategists develop the judgment crucial to making decisions about an uncertain future? It was the very question Knight had posed, but unlike Knight, Kahn had an answer: "ersatz experience." What strategists needed, he suggested, were "strange aids to thought," in the form of multiple imagined futures that could be developed through simulations such as war games and scenarios.

In 1961, Kahn left RAND to help found the Hudson Institute, where he eventually shared his ideas with Pierre Wack, an executive from Royal Dutch Shell. In the early 1970s Wack famously applied Kahn's ideas in the business world, by devising scenarios to help Shell prepare for what might take place as the oil-rich nations of the Middle East began to assert themselves on the world stage. When change did come, in the form of the price shocks induced by the 1973 OPEC oil embargo, Shell was able to ride the crisis out much better than its competitors. (In 1985, Wack chronicled Shell's efforts in two articles for this magazine: "Scenarios: Uncharted Waters Ahead" and "Scenarios: Shooting the Rapids.")

The Shell exercises marked the birth of scenario planning as a strategic tool for business managers. In subsequent years, Wack's successors at the company refined his method, and scenario planners from Shell went on to become some of the most prominent scholars and practitioners in the field. Nonetheless, few of the organizations that have conducted scenario-planning exercises in recent decades have institutionalized them as part of a broader effort to achieve strategic foresight.

One of the rare exceptions is the U.S. Coast Guard, which describes its work with scenario planning as part of a "cycle of strategic renewal." As such, it offers a model that many organizations can learn from.

One might ask how relevant the Coast Guard's experience is for businesses, but in fact it constitutes what social scientists call a "crucial-case test." As a military service, the Coast Guard has less organizational flexibility than most private firms, with a mission mandated by statute and a budget determined by Congress. What's more, for a long time its need to react daily to numerous emerging situations—from ships in distress to drug interdictions—forced it to focus almost exclusively on the short term, leaving it with little bandwidth to formulate strategy for the long term. Nevertheless, in recent years it has managed to leverage scenario planning to its advantage, reorienting the organization in an ongoing way toward the future. And that, in turn, has allowed it to respond and adapt to disruptive changes, such as those that followed the September 11 terrorist attacks.

Future-Proofing the Coast Guard

On that tragic morning, hundreds of thousands of people found themselves trapped in Lower Manhattan, desperate to escape the burning chaos that was Ground Zero. While some were able to walk uptown or across bridges, which officials had closed to vehicles, for many the best way off the island was by water. So over the next hours, an impromptu flotilla—of ferries, tugs, private craft, and fire and police boats—took clusters of people away from the wreckage of the World Trade Center and across the water to safety.

Although many vessels operated on their own initiative, a significant part of the evacuation was directed by the Coast Guard, which had issued a call for "all available boats" and coordinated the chaotic debarkation with remarkable poise, creativity, and efficiency. The effort reminded many of the storied British evacuation across the English Channel of several hundred thousand troops that Nazi forces had trapped in Dunkirk, on the coast of France.

That the Coast Guard rose to the challenge is no surprise. Although it has a broad set of responsibilities, ranging from search-and-rescue to environmental protection to port security, the organization's motto is *Semper paratus,* or "Always ready," and it prides itself on responding to emergencies. As one retired captain told me, "Our whole idea is, when the alarm goes off, to be able to fly into action."

But September 11 ended up being more than a short-term challenge. In its aftermath, the Coast Guard found its mission quickly expanding. Within a day it was tasked with implementing radically heightened port-security measures around the country: Port security had previously accounted for 1% to 2% of its daily operational load, but it soon consumed 50% to 60%. In March 2003 the Coast Guard was integrated into the new Department of Homeland Security, and that same month it was given the job of securing ports and waterways all over Iraq, following the U.S.-led invasion. In subsequent years the service's budget would double and its ranks would swell. A new future had arrived.

The Coast Guard adapted to this future nimbly—and did so in part because in the late 1990s it had conducted a scenario-planning exercise called Project Long View, which was designed to help the organization contend with "a startlingly complex future operating environment characterized by new or unfamiliar security threats." Its aim, in effect, was to future-proof the Coast Guard.

The service ran Long View in 1998 and 1999—and then, in 2003, in response to the shocks of September 11, renamed it Project Evergreen and began running it every four years. Ever since, the organization has relied on Evergreen to help its leaders think and act strategically.

Robust Strategy—No Matter What the Future Holds

When the Coast Guard decided to launch Long View, it enlisted the help of the Futures Strategy Group (FSG), a consultancy specializing in scenario planning. FSG maintains that uncertainty precludes prediction but demands anticipation—and that imaginatively and rigorously exploring plausible futures can facilitate decision-making.

Working with FSG, the Coast Guard identified four forces for change that would have a significant impact on its future: the role of the federal government, the strength of the U.S. economy, the seriousness of threats to U.S. society, and the demand for maritime services. By exploring them and looking forward some 20 years, the team came up with 16 possible "far-future worlds" in which the Coast Guard might have to operate. Of those, Coast Guard leaders selected five that were as distinct as possible from one another

The Future: A Glossary

MANAGING THE UNCERTAINTY of the future requires many tools, some of which have similar or even overlapping functions. To cut through the confusion, here's a brief guide.

- **Backcasting** asks participants to work backward in time from a particular future to ascertain what in the present caused its emergence. The practice is most often used to identify a path to a preferred future but can also be used to avoid steps toward a negative future. "Premortems," for example, aim to identify the causes of a hypothetical future failure.

- **Contingency Planning** aids decision-making by preparing participants for specific events that are considered possible or even likely. A contingency plan provides a playbook in case of emergency.

- **Crisis Simulations and Tabletop Exercises** have participants respond to specific scenarios and then analyze their actions, to help people prepare for real-life situations. They differ from war games in that they involve a specific possible future rather than a range of plausible futures.

- **Forecasting** involves making probabilistic predictions about the future and, as such, is a tool that practitioners of strategic foresight tend to avoid. But it, too, has its place in helping strategists manage uncertainty, adding a quantitative angle to the qualitative methods preferred by, say, scenario planners. The best approach is this: Predict what you can; imagine what you cannot; and develop the judgment to know the difference.

(while remaining plausible) and represented the range of environments the service might face. FSG then wrote detailed descriptions of those futures and the fictional events that led to them.

Each future world was given a name intended to capture its essence. "Taking on Water" described a future in which the U.S. economy struggled amid significant environmental degradation. In "Pax Americana," a humbled United States had to contend with a world rent by political instability and economic catastrophe. "Planet Enterprise" was dominated by giant transnational corporations. "Pan-American Highway" featured regional trade blocs oriented around the dollar and the euro. And "Balkanized America" presciently warned of a divided world in which "terrorism strikes with frightening frequency, and increasingly close to home."

- **Horizon Scanning** asks participants to search for "weak signals" of change in the present with an eye toward monitoring their development and assessing their potential impact. The practice is guided by the idea that the future often first comes into view in places that most of us are not paying attention to, such as specialized scientific journals.

- **Scenario Planning** uses stories about alternative futures to challenge assumptions and reframe perceptions of the present. The process does not attempt to predict the future but instead aims to explore plausible futures to inform strategy.

- **Trend Analysis** asks participants to consider the potential influence of patterns of change that are already visible. A popular structured approach is the STEEP framework, which disaggregates patterns of change into five categories: social, technological, economic, environmental, and political.

- **War Games** ask participants to engage an opponent in simulated conflict, often to explore reactions to novel circumstances. Like scenario planning, war games do not attempt to predict what will happen; rather, they project what could happen, thereby providing insight into decision-making. Despite the name, war games can address far more than just the military aspects of conflict.

Using those scenarios, the Coast Guard convened a three-day workshop, which FSG facilitated. Teams of civilians and officers were assigned to different future worlds and charged with devising strategies that would enable the Coast Guard to operate effectively in them. At the end of the workshop the teams compared notes on what they had come up with. Strategies that appeared again and again, across different teams, were deemed "robust." In their final report the organizers of Long View listed 10 of these strategies, ranging from the creation of a more unified command structure to the development of a more flexible human-resources system to the establishment of "full maritime domain awareness"—which the Coast Guard defines as the "ability to acquire, track, and identify in real time any vessel or aircraft entering America's maritime domain." All of these strategies, they argued, would help the Coast Guard carry out its mission, no matter what the future held.

Many of the strategies weren't novel. But Long View allowed participants to think about them in new ways that proved crucial in the post-September 11 world. In effect, Long View allowed the Coast Guard to pressure-test strategies under a range of plausible futures, prioritize the most-promising ones, and socialize them among the leadership— which meant that after the attacks, when the organization found its mission changing dramatically, it was able to respond quickly.

Launching Long View and subsequently establishing Evergreen as a continuous process wasn't easy. It took exceptionally strong leadership—in particular from admirals James Loy and Thad Allen. The program has also faced challenges in implementing ideas; there is a difference between strategic foresight and strategic execution. But once established, the program developed significant momentum, fueled in part by a growing cadre of alumni who saw the value of a dynamic relationship between the present and the future. The Coast Guard had institutionalized imagination.

Exploration Enables Exploitation

Long View and Evergreen weren't designed to bring about a wholesale organizational shift from the operational to the strategic or to train the Coast Guard's attention primarily on the long term. Instead, the goal was to get its personnel thinking about the future in a way that would inform and improve their ability to operate in the present.

That was no small challenge. Management scholars have long noted that, in order to survive and thrive over time, organizations need to both exploit existing competencies and explore new ones. They need to be "ambidextrous."

The problem is that those two imperatives compete for resources, demand distinct ways of thinking, and require different organizational structures. Doing one makes it harder to do the other. Ambidexterity requires managers to somehow resolve this paradox.

Long View and Evergreen helped the service's leaders do that. The programs didn't reduce the organization's ability to attend to the present. If anything, the opposite occurred. Exploration *enabled* exploitation.

The Coast Guard members I interviewed for my research reported that Long View and Evergreen accomplished this in several ways. At the most explicit level, they identified strategies that the Coast Guard then pursued. Take maritime domain awareness. The scenarios made it clear to Coast Guard leaders that in any plausible future, they would want the ability to identify and track every vessel in U.S. waters. Although this may seem like an obvious need, it's not a capability that the service had in the 1990s. As one retired admiral explained, "Ships could come in 10 miles off or even three miles off the United States' coast, and we might not know it." That was in part because U.S. agencies had no integrated system for gathering and disseminating information.

Even though the Coast Guard didn't have the organizational and technological infrastructure to establish full maritime domain awareness immediately, Long View built consensus about its value among top leadership, which helped the service implement it more quickly after 9/11. In fact, the Coast Guard captain who had managed Evergreen led the interagency effort to develop the first National Strategy for Maritime Security, which ultimately prompted the creation of the Nationwide Automatic Identification System—a sort of transponder system for ships.

The strategies that emerged from the scenario-planning exercises also enabled personnel who participated in them to act with a greater awareness of the service's future needs. For example, the first iteration of Evergreen stressed the importance of building strategic partnerships at home and abroad. With this in mind, one senior Coast Guard leader prepared for threats that might emerge in the Pacific by developing bilateral relationships with island nations there; sharing information, coordinating patrols, and holding joint exercises with counterparts in China, Russia, Canada, South Korea, and Japan; and finding ways to work more closely with other U.S. agencies, from the FBI to the National Oceanic and Atmospheric Administration.

At the most basic level, Long View and Evergreen simply got the service's people to think more about the future. The master chief petty officer of the Coast Guard Reserve described how Evergreen had changed his thinking, citing a recent conversation with a colleague: "He and I were here in my office this morning, talking about, 'Twenty-five years from now, what is the Coast Guard Reserve component going to look like?'" Before taking part in Evergreen, he added, "I just wouldn't understand how to think that way."

Perhaps most interesting, however—and most important in resolving the supposed paradox between exploration and exploitation—is the way that Long View and Evergreen helped participants understand the demands of the past and the future not as competing but as complementary. The exercises changed the very way in which participants thought about time.

Humans tend to conceive of time as linear and unidirectional, as moving from past to present to future, with each time frame discrete. We remember yesterday; we experience today; we anticipate tomorrow. But the best scenario planning embraces a decidedly non-linear conception of time. That's what Long View and Evergreen did: They took stock of trends in the present, jumped many years into the future, described plausible worlds created by those drivers, worked backward to develop stories about how those worlds had come to pass, and then worked forward again to develop robust strategies. In this model, time circles around on itself, in a constantly evolving feedback cycle between present and future. In a word, it is a loop.

Once participants began to view time as a loop, they understood *thinking about the future* as an essential component of *taking action in the present*. The scenarios gave them a structure that strengthened their ability to be strategic, despite tremendous uncertainty. It became clear that in making decisions, Coast Guard personnel should learn not only from past experience but also from imagined futures.

Getting Started

The prospect of organizing a scenario exercise can intimidate the uninitiated. There are distinct benefits to enlisting one of the individuals, boutique consultancies, or even large firms that specialize in scenarios to provide helpful direction. However, regardless of who runs the process, managers should follow these key guidelines:

Invite the right people to participate

One of the chief purposes of a scenario exercise is to challenge mental models of how the world works. To create the conditions for success, you'll need to bring together participants who have significantly different organizational roles, points of view, and personal experiences. You'll also need people who represent what Kees van der Heijden, one of Wack's successors at Shell, has described as the three powers necessary for any effective conversation about strategy: the power to perceive, the power to think, and the power to act.

Identify assumptions, drivers, and uncertainties

It's important to explicitly articulate the assumptions in your current strategy and what future you expect will result from its implementation. Think of this scenario as your projected scenario—but recognize that it's just one of many possible futures, and focus on determining which assumptions it would be helpful to revisit. Rafael Ramirez, who leads the Oxford Scenarios Programme, advises that in doing this you disaggregate *transactional actors,* which you can influence or control, from *environmental forces,* which you cannot. How might those forces combine to create different possible futures?

Imagine plausible, but dramatically different, futures

This can be the most difficult part of the exercise, particularly for those used to more analytical modes of thinking. Push yourself to imagine what the future will look like in five, 10, or even 20 years—without simply extrapolating from trends in the present. This takes a high degree of creativity and also requires the judgment to distinguish a scenario that, as the Coast Guard puts it, pushes the envelope of plausibility from one that tears it—an inherently subjective task. Good facilitators can both prime the imagination and maintain the guardrails of reality.

Inhabit those futures

Scenario planning is most effective when it's an immersive experience. Creating "artifacts from the future," such as fictional newspaper articles or even video clips, often helps challenge existing mental models. It's also a good idea to disconnect participants from the present, so hold workshops off-site and discourage the use of phones at them.

Isolate strategies that will be useful across multiple possible futures

Form teams to inhabit each of your far-future worlds, and give them this challenge: What should we be doing *now* that would enable us to operate better in that particular future? Create an atmosphere in which even junior participants can put forward ideas without hesitation. Once the groups develop strategies for their worlds, bring them together to compare notes. Look for commonalities, single them out, and identify plans and investments that will make sense across a range of futures.

Implement those strategies

This may sound obvious, but it is the place where most companies fall down. Using scenario planning to devise strategies isn't resource-intensive, but implementing them requires commitment. To couple foresight with action, leaders should set up a formal system in which managers have to explain explicitly how their plans will advance the firm's new strategies. Realistically, foresight will not drive every initiative, but scenario exercises can still be valuable in several ways. First, they can provide participants with a common language to talk about the future. Second, they can build support for an idea within an organization so that when the need for implementation becomes clear, it can move faster. Finally, they can enable participants to act at the unit level, even if the organization as a whole fails to link the present and future as tightly as it should.

Ingrain the process

In the long run you'll reap the greatest value from scenario exercises by establishing an iterative cycle—that is, a process that continually orients your organization toward the future while keeping an eye on the present, and vice versa. This ambidexterity will allow you to thrive under the best of conditions—and it's essential for survival under the worst. Moving in a loop between the present and multiple imagined futures helps you to adjust and update your strategies continually.

———————

This last point is critical. As the current pandemic has made clear, needs and assumptions can change quickly and unpredictably. Preparing for the future demands constant reappraisal. Strategic foresight—the capacity to sense, shape, and adapt to what happens—requires iterative exploration, whether through scenario planning or another method. (See "The Future: A Glossary," page 136.) Only by institutionalizing the imaginative process can organizations establish a continual give-and-take between the present and the future. Used dynamically in this way, scenario planning and other tools of strategic foresight allow us to map ever-shifting territory.

Of course, strategic foresight also enables us to identify opportunities and amplifies our ability to seize them. Organizations don't just prepare for the future. They make it. Moments of uncertainty hold great entrepreneurial potential. As Wack once wrote in these pages, "It is precisely in these contexts—not in stable times—that the real opportunities lie to gain competitive advantage through strategy."

It takes strength to stand up against the tyranny of the present and invest in imagination. Strategic foresight makes both possible—and offers leaders a chance for legacy. After all, they will be judged not only by what they do today but by how well they chart a course toward tomorrow.

Originally published in July–August 2020. Reprint R2004B

5 Ways to Stimulate Cash Flow in a Downturn

by Eddie Yoon and Christopher Lochhead

HISTORY TEACHES US VALUABLE LESSONS for managing cash during a nasty downturn. Companies that successfully navigated prior crises pursued cash-flow strategies that were both radically generous with customers and partners—and thoughtfully aggressive with near-term revenue and expense management.

These may seem like opposing ideas, but in reality they perfectly balance the empathy required to persuade customers to help while ensuring the economics of the business remain sound.

To achieve this balance, leaders can take five complementary actions:

1. Secure Sales by Taking Risks with Warranties, Guarantees, and Return Policies

Companies can secure near-term revenue by reassuring customers who are navigating a ton of uncertainty. Taking a risk with generous warranties and return policies can both calm nerves and close sales.

Hyundai demonstrated this successfully during the 2008 recession with its Assurance return program. The marketing campaign promised that if you lost your job soon after buying a Hyundai, the company would buy it back from you. Hyundai's market share grew from 3.1% to 4.3% in the first 10 months of 2009, and its sales grew nearly 24% the following year. It has introduced a similar version of the program during the current crisis.

2. Implement New Revenue and Pricing Models

Companies should test new revenue and pricing models with their most loyal customers, many of whom will jump at the chance to secure goods and services they know they will want and need at a meaningful discount.[1] This may require alternative pricing strategies like gift cards and subscriptions, as opposed to traditional transaction-based models.

Blaze Pizza, one of the market leaders in fast-casual pizza, recently launched a #BlazingItForward gift card campaign on social media and via its 2.4-million-member email list. During this promotion, someone who buys a $20 gift card gets a free pizza on their next purchase. Daniela Simpson, general manager of digital growth and head of marketing at Blaze, noted gift card sales have exceeded expectations. Gift cards can be tricky from an accounting and go-to-market standpoint, but note that Starbucks has 25 million mobile users who preload cash onto their rewards cards as an interest-free, negative working capital loan. In aggregate, this provides Starbucks with more than $1 billion in working capital.

Gift cards may seem like a retail-specific idea, but they are a tactic more companies should try. The travel and leisure segment, for example, could offer its best customers a way to secure their elite status for next year by forward-buying travel in bulk at a discount.

Remember that your "superconsumers" have a shared interest in your survival. While the revenue from these methods must be recognized over time, it does have meaningful benefits for your cash flow and balance sheet, as well as for forecasting. If you're a category or company that has toyed with the idea of migrating to subscription pricing, now is the time to try it. Companies that make the transition to subscription pricing may see their valuation multiples increase once the market stabilizes, given Wall Street's current affinity for subscription and "X as a service" business models.

3. Accelerate Innovation

Launch near-ready innovations in the pipeline now. Most companies are risk-averse regarding innovation, but just as generosity begets generosity, empathy begets empathy. Customers who typically may nitpick new innovations will be grateful for new and improved products or services—even if they're released before all the kinks are worked out. Those customers likely will help you identify problems and fix them before a broader rollout.

This is what Tesla is doing effectively with its autopilot software. The software is not finished, but Tesla knows that the best way to improve it is to gather actual data from drivers using it in the wild.

Other companies are simply moving up launch dates to help consumers hungry for distractions. ESPN, for example, accelerated the launch of *The Last Dance*, its highly anticipated Michael Jordan documentary, from June to April. Many Hollywood studios, on the other hand, are making the mistake of delaying launches to maximize mass market revenue, missing the opportunity to launch their movies as high-priced, pay-per-view events.

4. Cut "Sacred Cow" Marketing Costs

Take a swing at marketing costs that are suspected to not pay back but are too politically difficult to cut during better times. Often these are hard-to-measure marketing costs, or they're geared toward motivating distributors or channel partners more than consumers.

A good example of this is when, back in 2009, Anheuser-Busch InBev cut a number of sports sponsorships (including Manchester United and exclusivity on the Winter Olympics) that motivated distributors but had little evidence of customer awareness or impact.

5. Engage in New Kinds of Customer Acquisition

Finally, companies should seek to proactively acquire customers during this crisis. One of the best ways to do it is through strategic sampling. This is especially true of companies that sell intellectual property, like software, training, and services, which have low marginal costs. Zoom has generated a lot of attention by offering its services to K-12 education for free.[2] These investments enhance its brand over the long term, and may convert people into paying customers six to 12 months down the line.

Another way to drive customer acquisition is via M&A. Valuations are as low as they've been in a while, so companies with the means should be aggressively shopping for acquisitions that bring over new customers, cross-selling opportunities, or new business models and categories. Consider the New York Times Company, which just acquired Audm, a subscription-based audio app that offers long-form journalism read aloud by celebrated audiobook narrators.[3] Given that print is migrating toward podcasts, this is a great time to make a bet for the future on the cheap.

Companies need to resist the temptation to stay hunkered down on defense during these difficult times. Instead, go on the offense by using radical generosity and thoughtful aggressiveness as guiding principles. Dark times are when legendary companies and leaders are forged.

Originally published April 4, 2020. Reprint H05JEH

Notes

1. Eddie Yoon, Steve Carlotti, and Dennis Moore, "Make Your Best Customers Even Better," hbr.org, March 1, 2014, https://store.hbr.org/product/make-your-best-customers-even-better/f1403a?sku=F1403A-PDF-ENG.

2. Jordan Novat, "Why Zoom Has Become the Darling of Remote Workers During the COVID-19 Crisis," cnbc.com, March 21, 2020, https://www.cnbc.com/2020/03/21/why-zoom-has-become-darling-of-remote-workers-amid-covid-19-outbreak.html.

3. Nicholas Quah, "Is The New York Times' Purchase of Audm a Turning Point in Its New Audio Strategy?" NiemanLab, March 24, 2020, https://www.niemanlab.org/2020/03/is-the-new-york-times-purchase-of-audm-a-turning-point-in-its-new-audio-strategy/.

The Case for M&A in a Downturn

by Brian Salsberg

DURING A CRISIS, BUSINESSES should be examining their existing lists of potential acquisition targets and should be preparing to act, as deal premiums are likely to come down and assets that companies had been reluctant to sell may become available.

But the window for maximizing value could be relatively short, if history is any indication.

Learning from the Global Financial Crisis

Evidence from the global financial crisis (GFC) of late 2007 through early 2009 shows that companies that made significant acquisitions during the economic downturn outperformed those that did not.

There are some caveats: The GFC was, as its name indicates, a financial crisis, and was somewhat limited to the financial services and real estate sectors. Governments needed to bail out banks as many companies were overextended. Consumers were crunched as the value of their homes dropped dramatically and some found their mortgages underwater.

Today almost the entire services sector of the economy is immobilized and unemployment is at a much higher level after the 2008 recession. The Covid-19 crisis is first and foremost a health crisis, and the spread of the disease is likely to be the key factor in determining the length of the downturn, and thus the optimal M&A window. Still, the GFC is the best modern example we can look to when predicting the ultimate shape of the recovery from an M&A perspective.

With regard to deal making, the recovery beginning in 2009 was very much U-shaped. That is, it took more than five years for deal volume to recover to average pre-crisis levels, and deal value never quite recovered. (See figure 13-1.)

The story regarding deal multiples—defined as enterprise value divided by EBITDA (earnings before interest, taxes, depreciation, and amortization)—was somewhat different, with much more of a V-shaped recovery. Deal values plummeted from an average of 10.8x in the three years before the 2008 crisis to as low as 6.5x in 2009, before rebounding to the 10-year average of 11.6x by 2019. (See figure 13-2.)

History suggests, therefore, that there will be a relatively short M&A window that opens as the Covid-19 crisis ends, during which bargains will be had by those who have the liquidity and the risk tolerance to move quickly, and who have done their homework in advance.

Active Acquirers May Outperform

There are some qualifiers to consider when examining the data.

First, there can never be a true control in the M&A world to measure against—a company either does a deal or does not. Additionally, company performance as measured by total shareholder return (TSR) is the result of a mix of inorganic and organic activities, as well as any number of external factors, none of which can be totally isolated.

That said, we nevertheless can conclude the following:

- Those companies that made acquisitions totaling at least 10% of their market cap from 2008 through 2010 (active acquirers) had an average TSR of 6.4% from January 2007 through January 2008, compared with a TSR of -3.4% for less active companies. (See figure 13-3.) A similar difference was seen in median TSR.

- The trend continued over the period of January 2007 through January 2010, when average TSR was 10.5% for active acquirers and 3.3% for less active companies.

FIGURE 13-1

Global M&A deals, 2000–2019

*During the 2008 financial crisis, the **number of M&A deals** dipped by almost 31% year-over-year . . .*

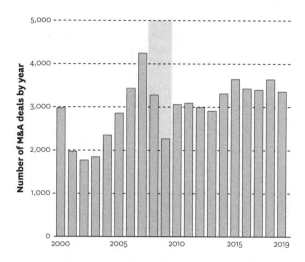

*. . . and the **value of those deals** fell by about 27% in the same time period. Similar drops are possible due to Covid-19.*

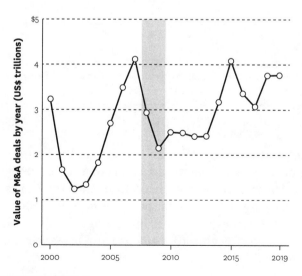

Source: EY analysis and Dealogic.
Note: Excludes real estate acquisitions. Volume based on deals of US$100 million or more.

FIGURE 13-2

Deal multiples, 2000–2020

An examination of deal multiples—the ratio of enterprise value divided by EBITDA that is used to determine a company's value—during the 2008 financial crisis suggests that valuations that have or will decline during the current downturn are likely to bounce back somewhat quickly.

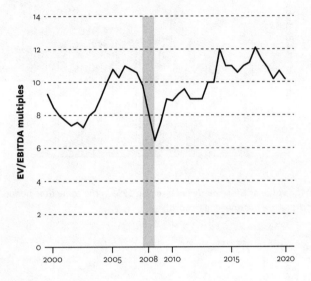

Source: EY analysis and Dealogic.
Note: EBITDA—short for "earnings before interest, taxes, depreciation, and amortization"—is a measure of a company's financial performance.

TSR for active acquirers with strong liquidity positions (cash and short-term investments to revenue of at least 7.0% in 2007) increased by an average of 5%. In contrast, other companies saw an average increase of 1.7% over the period from January 2007 through January 2010. This gap continued in the long term (five years), with active acquirers' TSR growing at an average of 16.9% versus 4.9% for other companies.

FIGURE 13-3

Total shareholder return (TSR) growth by acquirer type, 2007–2010

Firms that made significant acquisitions during the 2008 financial crisis outper-formed those that did not.

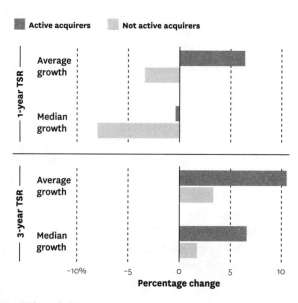

Source: EY analysis, Capital IQ, *Fortune*.
Note: Analysis of companies on the 2008 *Fortune* 1,000 list; excludes financial services, real estate, and companies where the share price was unavailable on January 1, 2007, and January 1, 2012.

Deal Activity May Be the Best Option for Excess Liquidity

Companies with excess liquidity may find that shareholders and boards are more conservative about how this liquidity is used. Specifically, share buybacks and possibly dividend payments may be curtailed for several years and companies will need to keep a higher level of cash on hand. These factors will require them to use any excess cash to generate long-term shareholder value.

At the same time, with a focus on preserving jobs and the health of the economy, governments and regulators are likely to be much more tolerant of larger acquisitions in many industries.

EY analysis suggests it is not too soon to consider M&A opportunities and prepare to act. CEOs, CFOs, and heads of strategy and corporate development need to think carefully about the "new normal" and which acquisitions would be accretive to their current business models. There are a few areas in the deal process that will no longer operate as usual, particularly during this period of social distancing. Companies thinking about M&A will need to consider these unique aspects of getting a deal done, including:

- **Transaction diligence.** Even if the majority of diligence can be performed remotely, it is likely to take longer. Diligence requiring on-site visits, such as to physical plants, is much more difficult to do via video. Boards may be reluctant to approve an asset or operations-heavy transaction without an actual site visit. Pressure-testing the strength of the balance sheet and forecasting expected cash flows for the next 12 to 24 months will be more critical than ever. Additionally, cyber diligence (that is, assessing the strength of the target's IT vulnerability) will increasingly become a focus area due to the accelerating reliance on technology.

- **Synergy modeling.** This process will need to be conducted with an eye toward the new normal. For instance, resilient supply chains have more redundancies than efficient supply chains, meaning they are more expensive and have fewer opportunities to cut costs and achieve synergies.

- **Business models.** In our new normal, companies' business models are likely to change, and not just in obvious ways. For example, that hot new kombucha beverage with all the social media hype may struggle to find a space on retail shelves when grocery channels begin prioritizing established brands and safety stock.

- **Post-acquisition integration.** Maintaining employee morale and engagement is critical, especially in this environment. Many people will be focused on their job security, so asking them to put their energy toward onboarding target employees may be difficult. While it is possible to work your way through much of the integration playbook remotely, culture and change management aspects can be tricky to communicate over videoconference. Being considerate of working hours, ensuring various integration meetings stick to a reasonable time frame, and infusing the process with the appropriate amount of ice-breaker activities (such as virtual happy hours) are some ways to ease the burden of the work-from-home context.

Ultimately, planning for M&A in the near future will require significant rigor. Companies must understand the recovery curve scenarios that target firms are likely to experience coming out of the crisis, in addition to understanding the true liquidity situation of the target and any of the target's near-term CAPEX or similar needs.

Note

Special thanks to Rahul Agrawal, Manvi Gupta, Banipreet Kaur, and Vaishali Madaan for their contributions to this article.

Originally published May 17, 2020. Reprint H05MDM

In a Downturn, Include Your Employees in Cost-Cutting Decisions

by Patrick Daoust and Paul Simon

ALMOST EVERY BUSINESS IS REORGANIZING its operations in response to the economic slowdown caused by the Covid-19 pandemic. Often, companies take a top-down approach to resizing based on a limited set of data such as earnings forecasts and competitive benchmarking. But following this playbook usually results in "wrong sizing" and demoralized employees.

Instead, leaders should redesign their operations based on data provided by their most valuable sources of proprietary insights— their employees. Democratizing the collection of data and recommendations allows leadership teams to gain a much clearer picture of activities and initiatives underway within their organizations. It also offers a clearer lens for evaluating which activities are the most valuable to strategic objectives and which can be automated or managed in a shared services environment—or ceased.

When leaders take this bottom-up approach, we have found they not only cut costs significantly but also realize their goals more rapidly because managers and employees are motivated to help. Changes are then more likely to stick.

One fast-food restaurant chain supplemented its leadership team's top-down analysis with qualitative and quantitative data from vice presidents, directors, and employees, which allowed it to reduce its sales, general, and administration costs by more than one-third and refocus on core strategic areas, such as marketing, product innovation, and new franchises. Likewise, a hospital group uncovered ways to improve clinical and administrative team interactions, making it possible to treat more patients across specialties while reducing operating costs by more than 20%.

In both cases, leadership teams were able to transform their companies because they based decisions on more accurate information. But how can leaders be sure they are collecting the data they need?

Below, we recommend focusing on four types of information:

1. Key Routines and Projects

The first step in redesigning a company is for the leadership team to ask each division or function head to create a list of 20 to 30 routines and projects that are fundamentally important to the company. Routines are repetitive by nature and can range from the daily to the quarterly. Projects, such as the deployment of a new support system or the launch of a new service line, have a specified beginning and end.

Gathering this data can enable a company's leadership team to see the activities and projects underway at a more granular level, making it possible to spot gaps and redundancies quickly. For example, one company we worked with discovered several hundred of its global sales and marketing employees attended conferences to sell products despite low success rates. Another found salespeople repeatedly visited the same client because sales forces were not coordinated. Yet another leadership team uncovered that three times as many IT projects were underway than had been budgeted for. And on and on.

2. Effort Required

To help a leadership team better understand the effort required for every routine and project, division heads should hold workshops with their managers to discuss the volume and nature of the work involved.

Operational data supplied by employees permits leadership teams to precisely evaluate which routines require more or less support. One leadership team may discover armies of people are executing the same basic support tasks after a series of acquisitions—like IT, human resources, legal, finance, and government relations. Or, at the other end of the spectrum, more people may be needed to carry out critical responsibilities. For example, food and pharmacy retailers may have to ramp up staff to fill and deliver online orders, which have soared from 5% to nearly 40% of many companies' sales during the pandemic.

3. Strategic Priorities

After this exercise, division heads should ask managers to work with employees to tag identified routines and projects based on the strategic priorities of the company and their own division. These tags should be sorted into three categories: *core, context,* and *cease.*

Core routines and projects are a company's top priorities. These are capabilities that companies may want to invest in to differentiate themselves from the competition and to spur future growth. They might include research and development in the pharmaceutical industry, design in the fashion industry, customer experience in retail, and capital expenditure management in heavy industries like transportation and manufacturing.

By contrast, context routines are standard services and activities that can be deprioritized and optimized to be more efficient, often by sharing or automating services. For example, managers at one retailer pointed out that a single team could scout the world for new fashion trends in men's shoes, women's shoes, and accessories—instead of sending a separate team for each product. One HR department's recruiting function suggested a chatbot could handle basic questions and answers from online job applicants, freeing up employees to focus on the interview and hiring process and speeding up the pace of hiring.

Other routines should be categorized as cease if they are adding little value or are no longer relevant to the company's strategy. For example, one retailer halted the preparation and distribution of most of its management reports by the finance function. Only a few managers found them useful, yet they took up most of the team's time and effort. A pharmaceutical company identified unprofitable product lines that could be retired, freeing up about 40% of the research team's time to develop new products.

4. New Operating Model Ideas

Next, leadership teams should empower division heads to work with managers and employees to redesign their operations. This should start with pinpointing which capabilities need be built up in order for the company to bounce back and grow. Managers should crowdsource not just the operational data they think they need to achieve new efficiencies, but also innovative ideas for reinventing their operations and their offerings for the future.

By including this data from employees in the process, leadership teams can pursue more ambitious visions, since they will have both the significant savings and the talent they need to execute their plans. Retailers will be able to pivot and offer much more elaborate shopping experiences online, complete with "magic mirrors" that let customers virtually try on shoes or apparel and details about which store has the product in stock. Grocers and pharmacies can invest in digital networks that allow them to nimbly redeploy their workforces by sending alerts when there is an opening for someone to work in a different store, branch, or stockroom. Transportation companies can reallocate their scarce resources toward developing more efficient ways to deliver packages from warehouses to customers' homes. And pharmaceutical companies can ensure a brighter future by developing new products and services at a faster pace, transforming innovations like new vaccines or treatments into the bread-and-butter products of tomorrow.

By tapping into data provided by managers and employees to redesign a company, leadership teams will not only be able to make better decisions—they will also be able to improve their operations, and still have workforces engaged and motivated to continuously improve them.

Originally published May 5, 2020. Reprint H05L18

Preparing Your Business for a Post-Pandemic World

by Carsten Lund Pedersen and Thomas Ritter

ALONG WITH THE SEVERE HEALTH and humanitarian crisis caused by the coronavirus pandemic, executives around the world face enormous business challenges: the collapse of customer demand, significant regulatory modifications, supply chain interruptions, unemployment, economic recession, and increased uncertainty. And like the health and humanitarian sides of the crisis, the business side needs ways to recover. Ad hoc responses won't work; organizations must lay the groundwork for their recoveries now.

The management theorist Henry Mintzberg famously defined strategy as 5 Ps: plan, ploy, pattern, position, and perspective. We have adapted his framework to propose our own 5 Ps for responding to the crisis: position, plan, perspective, projects, and preparedness. The following questions can guide you as you work to bounce back.

1. What Position Can You Attain During and After the Pandemic?

To make smart strategic decisions, you must understand your organization's *position* in your environment. Who are you in your market, what role do you play in your ecosystem, and who are your main competitors? You must also understand where you are headed. Can you shut down your operations and reopen unchanged after the pandemic? Can you regain lost ground? Will you be bankrupt, or can you emerge as a market leader fueled by developments during the lockdown?

We hear of many firms that are questioning their post-pandemic viability, including those in the travel, hospitality, and events industries. We also hear of firms accelerating their growth because their value propositions are in high demand; think of home office equipment, internet-enabled communication and collaboration tools, and home delivery services. Because of such factors, firms will differ in their resilience. You should take steps now to map your probable position when the pandemic eases.

2. What Is Your Plan for Bouncing Back?

A *plan* is a course of action pointing the way to the position you hope to attain. It should explicate what you need to do *today* to achieve your objectives *tomorrow*. In the current context, the question is what you must do to get through the crisis and return to business as usual when it ends.

The lack of a plan will only exacerbate your company's disorientation in an already confusing situation. When drawing up the steps you intend to follow, think broadly and deeply, and take a long view.

3. How Will Your Culture and Identity Change?

Perspective means the way an organization sees the world and itself. In all likelihood, your culture and identity will change as a result of the pandemic. A crisis can bring people together and facilitate a collective spirit of endurance—but it can also push people apart, with individuals distrusting one another and predominantly looking after themselves. It's crucial to consider how your perspective might evolve. How culturally prepared was your organization to deal with the crisis? Will the ongoing situation bring your employees together or drive them apart? Will they see the organization differently when this is over? Your answers will inform what you can achieve when the pandemic ends.

4. What New Projects Do You Need to Launch, Run, and Coordinate?

Your answer to this question should point you toward a set of *projects* for tackling your coronavirus-related problems. The challenge is to prioritize and coordinate initiatives that will future-proof the organization. Beware of starting numerous projects that all depend on the same critical resources, which might be specific individuals, such as top managers, or specific departments, such as IT. If you have too many new initiatives, you could end up with a war over resources that delays or derails your strategic response.

5. How Prepared Are You to Execute Your Plans and Projects?

Finally, you need to assess your organization's *preparedness*. Are you ready and able to accomplish the projects you've outlined, particularly if much of your organization has shifted to remote work? We see big differences in preparedness at the individual, team, organization, and national levels. The resources at hand, along with the speed and quality of decision-making processes, vary greatly, and the differences will determine who achieves success and who falls short of it.

Be aware that consumers will remember how you reacted during the crisis. Raising prices during a shortage, for example, could have a significant effect on your customer relationships going forward.

The coronavirus has had unprecedented impacts on the world—and the worst is yet to come. Companies must act today if they are to bounce back in the future. Doing so will help the world as a whole recover—and, we hope, become more resilient in the process.

Originally published April 10, 2020. Reprint H05JNP

About the Contributors

JAMES ALLEN is a senior partner in Bain's London office and a co-leader of its global strategy practice. He is the coauthor of several books, including *The Founder's Mentality: How to Overcome the Predictable Crises of Growth* (Harvard Business Review Press, 2016).

JANET BANKS is a former managing director at FleetBoston Financial and a former vice president at Chase Manhattan Bank, responsible for leadership development and succession planning. She's been an executive coach, an organizational consultant, and an executive search consultant.

TIM BREENE was the CEO of Accenture Interactive and is the CEO of the World Relief. He is the coauthor of *Jumping the S-Curve: How to Beat the Growth Cycle, Get on Top, and Stay There* (Harvard Business Review Press, 2011).

DIANE COUTU was a communications specialist at McKinsey & Company and an affiliate scholar and Julius Silberger Fellow at the Boston Psychoanalytic Society and Institute.

PATRICK DAOUST is a partner in the operations practice of Oliver Wyman.

WALTER FRICK is Deputy Editor of HBR.org.

RAJ GUPTA was the chairman of Rohm and Haas and has served on the boards of Hewlett-Packard, The Vanguard Group, Tyco International, and Delphi Automotive.

SHALENE GUPTA is a research associate at Harvard Business School.

STEPHEN HEIDARI-ROBINSON was British Prime Minister David Cameron's adviser on energy and the environment. He was a leader in McKinsey's organization practice, and he is a coauthor of *ReOrg: How to Get It Right* (Harvard Business Review Press, 2016).

SUZANNE HEYWOOD is the managing director of Exor Group. She was a leader in McKinsey's organization practice, and she is a coauthor of *ReOrg: How to Get It Right* (Harvard Business Review Press, 2016).

CHRISTOPHER LOCHHEAD is a coauthor of *Niche Down and Play Bigger* and the host of the podcasts *Follow Your Different* and *Lochhead on Marketing*. He has been an adviser to over 50 venture-backed tech companies and a former chief marketing officer at three public tech firms.

JOSHUA D. MARGOLIS is an associate professor of business administration at Harvard Business School.

PAUL NUNES is Global Managing Director of Thought Leadership for Accenture Research. He is the coauthor of *Jumping the S-Curve: How to Beat the Growth Cycle, Get on Top, and Stay There* (Harvard Business Review Press, 2011).

CARSTEN LUND PEDERSEN is an assistant professor in the department of marketing at Copenhagen Business School, where he researches B2B digitization strategies, employee autonomy, and market strategies in times of change.

DAVID RHODES is a senior partner and managing director in the Boston Consulting Group's London office.

THOMAS RITTER is a professor of market strategy and business development in the department of strategy and innovation at Copenhagen Business School, where he researches business model innovation, market strategies, and market management.

BRIAN SALSBERG is the Global Buy and Integrate Leader for EY, leading fully integrated M&A management services across sectors. He has experience working directly with CEOs, executives, business teams, boards of directors, and PE-backed companies in all facets of strategic planning, due diligence, corporate development, and M&A.

J. PETER SCOBLIC is a cofounder and principal of Event Horizon Strategies, a foresight consultancy, and a senior fellow in the International Security Program at New America. He received a doctorate from Harvard Business School, where his work on strategy and uncertainty won the Wyss Award for Excellence in Doctoral Research.

PAUL SIMON is a senior consultant at Oliver Wyman.

DANIEL STELTER is the founder of the German think tank Beyond the Obvious. He was a senior partner and managing director in BCG's Berlin office and the global leader of the firm's corporate development practice area.

PAUL G. STOLTZ is the founder and CEO of PEAK Learning, a global research and consulting firm based in San Luis Obispo, California.

SANDRA J. SUCHER is the Joseph L. Rice III Faculty Fellow and a professor of management practice at Harvard Business School.

ROBERT I. SUTTON is a professor of management science and engineering at Stanford University, where he cofounded the Hasso Plattner Institute of Design and the Stanford Technology Ventures Program. He is the author of *The No-Asshole Rule*.

EDDIE YOON is the founder of Eddie Would Grow, a think tank and advisory firm on growth strategy for VC- and PE-backed, high-growth companies. His book, *Superconsumers*, was published by Harvard Business Review Press in 2016.

CHRIS ZOOK is a partner in Bain & Company's Boston office and a coleader of its global strategy practice. He is the coauthor of several books, including *The Founder's Mentality: How to Overcome the Predictable Crises of Growth* (Harvard Business Review Press, 2016).

Index